SYBASE® SYSTEM XI
PERFORMANCE TUNING STRATEGIES

Ronald A. Phillips
Bonnie K. O'Neil
Marshall Brain

For book and bookstore information

http://www.prenhall.com

Prentice Hall PTR
Upper Saddle River, New Jersey 07458

Editorial/production supervision: *Craig Little*
Cover design: *Design Source*
Cover design director: *Jerry Votta*
Manufacturing manager: *Alexis R. Heydt*
Acquisitions editor: *Mike Meehan*

The publisher offers discounts on this book when ordered in bulk quantities.
For more information, contact:

Corporate Sales Department
Prentice Hall PTR
1 Lake Street
Upper Saddle River, NJ 07458

Phone: 800-382-3419
Fax: 201-236-7141
E-mail: corpsales@prenhall.com

Printed in the United States of America
10 9 8 7 6 5 4 3 2 1

ISBN 0-13-494865-3

Prentice-Hall International (UK) Limited, *London*
Prentice-Hall of Australia Pty. Limited, *Sydney*
Prentice-Hall Canada Inc., *Toronto*
Prentice-Hall Hispanoamericana, S.A., *Mexico*
Prentice-Hall of India Private Limited, *New Delhi*
Prentice-Hall of Japan, Inc., *Tokyo*
Simon & Schuster Asia Pte. Ltd., *Singapore*
Editora Prentice-Hall do Brasil, Ltda., *Rio de Janeiro*

CONTENTS

PREFACE

Just about any technical shop can load Sybase System XI on a machine and develop a client/server database application with it. If the database is simple (50 or so tables), small (a few megabytes), and lightly loaded (two or three users), then the application will work well. Unfortunately, it is very likely that the system will die once you try to scale it up to a production system. For example, if you increase the number of users to 100 or the data size to a gigabyte, the system will generally collapse under its own weight. While it is simple to design a prototype database, it is much harder to design a database that works well under the heavy load seen in a normal production environment.

The goal of this book is to teach you, in as tight and succinct a way as possible, the essential techniques needed to create high-performance production databases in a client/server environment. Before you can become a true server engineer you have to know the quintessential truths discussed in this book. Without this knowledge, your systems will flounder.

This book is not for beginners. It assumes that you already know something about SQL and perhaps have created one or two databases. It is also not a replacement for the Sybase performance book that comes with the Sybase server. This book is instead a condensation of many years of combined performance tuning experience into a volume that you can read and master very quickly.

Databases, at their heart, are extremely simple. As described in Chapter 1, they contain just a few basic elements that are repeated and combined in hundreds of ways. Because the elements are so simple, much of what you read in this book will seem like common sense once you have read it. The interesting point is that it takes most people up to a decade to gain these insights. Although the techniques make intuitive sense, they are very hard to grasp unless you have the perspective gained from many years of experience. In this book, the masters unveil their secrets for your immediate consumption.

Organization

This book contains nine chapters, each directed at a specific performance tuning area.

Chapter 1 introduces you to the field of performance tuning and sets the framework for discussion throughout the rest of the book. This chapter describes the essential performance tuning areas, lays out a sample database, and describes basic techniques.

Chapter 2 discusses database design and focuses on the conceptual, logical and physical modeling phases. This chapter demonstrates how to design performance into a database from the start.

Chapter 3 covers the optimizer. Each query that you write may or may not perform well, depending on how the optimizer interprets it. This chapter shows you how to understand and modify the optimizer's decisions.

Chapter 4 demonstrates an essential technique called execution thread analysis. Using this two-phase methodology you can find and repair performance problems in any production database.

Chapter 5 discusses indexes and index design, showing you both the good and bad attributes of indexes and helping you to understand how they can both improve and degrade performance.

Chapter 6 covers locking and concurrency issues, which are often an important but hidden contributor to performance degradation. Because the server manages locks automatically, it is very easy to miss them when trying to isolate a problem. This chapter reveals the servers locking mechanisms so that you can design maximum concurrency into your database from the start.

Chapters 7 and 8 demonstrate essential strategies, tactics and techniques that every performance tuner should understand and use consistently.

Chapter 9 finishes the book by discussing memory and caching. More memory will almost always improve performance in some way, but by understanding the role of memory in the performance equation you can often obtain much more significant results.

About the Authors

Ron Phillips is a Principle Consultant for dbINTELLECT (rphillips@dbintellect.com). He has over 15 years of experience in a variety of computer environments and database systems. Since 1987 he has concentrated on the development and implementation of super large scale databases using Sybase, Oracle, and Informix. He specializes in Data Modeling, Business Rule Analysis, Performance Tuning, and the development of sound DBA methods and techniques that facilitate high performance data centric Client/Server environments.

Bonnie O'Neil serves as a Senior Principal Management Consultant for Miaco Corporation (boneil@miaco.com). She has over eleven years of experience in database management systems, including four major database designs, and specializes in data modeling, design (including data warehousing), business rules and client/server architecture. Her emphasis and pioneering work as a leading expert in business rules is recognized throughout the industry. She also mentors new installations, advising the DBA staff how to expertly manage relational databases.

Marshall Brain is the President of Interface Technologies, Inc. (http://www.iftech.com). As the author of six books on Visual C++, Windows NT and Motif application development, as well as the web's popular On-Line Training Center, he has helped hundreds of thousands of readers rapidly master a variety of development environments. He has 10 years of training and high-end object oriented application development experience. He has previously taught in the North Carolina State University Computer Science department, where he is a member of the Academy of Outstanding Teachers.

Acknowledgments

The authors wish to thank the following people for their significant and unselfish contributions to this book.

Steve Maier of Sybase North American Sales (sml@sybase.com) has been instrumental throughout the entire development process. His advice, suggestions and reviews have tremendously improved the quality of this book.

Eduard Mosert of dbINTELLECT (emosert@dbintellect.com) is a high-level DBA who helped with script creation, testing and proofing. Without his efforts most of the examples would not exist.

We owe a debt of gratitude to Paul Hoyt of dbINTELLECT for his encouragement and support.

Our editor Mike Meehan shepherded this project though Prentice Hall, and without his persistence this book would not exist.

A special thanks to Leigh Ann Brain for layout services and support, and to Barbara Phillips and Perry O'Neil for their patience and understanding, and to Cindy for her globs.

INTRODUCTION

This chapter introduces the reader to the fundamentals of performance tuning, laying a conceptual framework that allows development of the database tuning methodology. It shows the reader how to use the business model as a foundation document to define the performance requirements for the application. It also discusses a more general problem: what do you do when you are stuck with a client/server system that has poor performance, and how do you approach the solution process?

1.1 The Problem

If you have been in the database business for any length of time, then you are likely to be familiar with the development process for "Client/Server Database Applications." Let's follow the process from a DBA's perspective. Typically the process starts with a requirements specification that in turn yields a database design. Code generation and system testing follow. After spending hundreds of thousands of dollars on hardware, software, programmers' salaries, high priced consultants, training, etc., the development team moves the system into a production setting and the database sees its first real users.

Furthermore, you would be familiar with what happens next. Approximately one week to a month later a bomb drops: Performance is ABYSMAL!

As real users in real numbers begin to load the system with real data, the system collapses under its own weight until it is unusable. The crisis begins.

In many development environments this sort of crisis is inevitable. Either through a lack of experience or a lack of foresight, most designers and project managers do not begin to consider performance issues until an application goes production and users are screaming. There are occasional exceptions: For example, a database designer might slightly denormalize a design in the name of performance. In practice, however, it is generally the case that performance tuning is an afterthought. Tuning is something to be done after the system is already in production and found to be performing poorly.

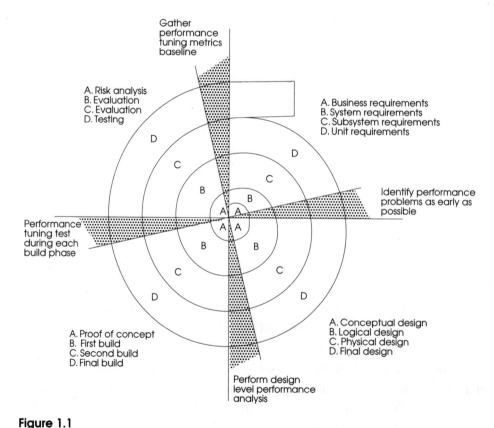

Figure 1.1

The System Development Lifecycle. Read around the spiral starting at the innermost "A."

The authors of this book believe that performance is an integral part of the overall development strategy. Performance should be built into the system in every phase of the system development lifecycle. See Figure 1.1. By taking this approach, designers not only prevent the crises that poor performance causes in a production environment, but also give themselves the opportunity to create much more stable and reliable systems over the lifetime of the project. This book develops a strategic approach that allows developers to craft high performance systems from the very beginning, before any code is written. Performance becomes a part of the overall design and plan, rather than an afterthought.

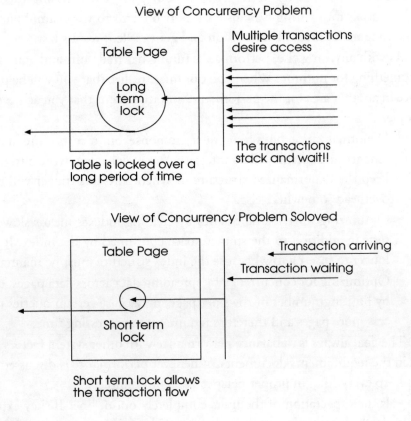

Figure 1.2

Concurrency Problem and Solution

Concurrency is a primary component of this strategic approach. In our travels, we have found innumerable applications developed with no prior understanding of concurrency or any sort of plan for dealing with its affects on system performance. Many problems in multi-user, high-volume client/server applications directly relate to the contention arising from the many activities taking place naturally and simultaneously in a database. See Figure 1.2. The strategy and tactics described in this book demonstrate how developers can incorporate execution thread analysis and transaction maps into their development environment and produce code which takes these factors into account proactively rather than reactively.

In addition, the book outlines a systematic tuning methodology that you can use to troubleshoot existing applications. You can use this methodology to ferret out the most costly bottlenecks in your system first. Using execution thread analysis for existing systems enables two teams to work simultaneously to fine-tune major areas of contention and get excellent results fast.

As with anything else, performance tuning has trade-offs and you cannot get something for nothing. When you optimize, realize that you will be paying a price in another area for the performance improvements that you achieve. For example:

- Denormalization buys faster query response, but it costs more in maintenance and sacrifices data integrity. You may have to write a trigger to keep the denormalized structure in synch, and this trigger will create overhead somewhere else.
- Optimizing for retrieval queries by creating indexes means slower inserts in addition to the storage space consumed by the index. It takes longer to insert a row because the index structure must be maintained.
- Optimizing for concurrency by spreading data across data pages, thereby limiting number of rows per page, may cause certain queries to access more pages and therefore require more processing time.

The goal always is to balance performance with other system factors specified in the requirements documents. Whenever performance is discussed, you must keep everything in proper perspective. For example:

- Is the expectation of the users completely out of line? If they expect a database to retrieve 2 million rows with instantaneous response time then perhaps the requirements need derating.

- Are users expecting the same performance from a client/server system that they are getting on a customized mainframe application that uses a raw disk/file system devoid of any of the overhead of a DataBase Management System (DBMS)? If so, evaluate why you are using a DBMS. Features such as flexibility, security, integrity, and recoverability are usually worth the trade-off, but verify this in advance.

You must learn to help your customers set realistic expectations up front, before they take delivery of the system. The time to set these expectations is in the requirements phase rather than at delivery. The business rules that you gather in the requirements phase should specify exactly how long different operations should take.

1.2 Understanding the Components of the Performance Problem

Client/server systems are especially complex because they have many interrelated components. See Figure 1.3. Any particular performance problem may result from a specific component or from an interaction between multiple components.

The Sybase System XI Performance and Tuning Guide recognizes the following components and layers as performance enablers:

1. The Client Application

2. The Database design

3. The SQL Server

4. Client Hardware

5. Network Parameters (bit rate, loading, etc.)

6. Server Hardware

7. The Operating System

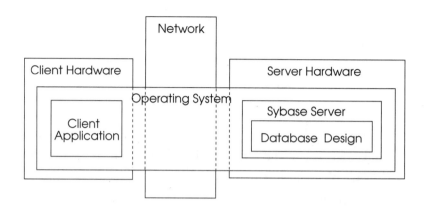

Figure 1.3

Client/Server Interrelated Performance Tuning Components

Although you should be aware of all these components, this book will concentrate on the first three. You need to know the limitations of your given configuration, such as hardware, software, and network. You need to know if you can help performance by adding CPUs or memory. However, these are not performance tuning issues per se—they are systems issues and should be handled by systems professionals. Any client/server environment should have a network engineer. He or she can recommend approaches for increasing throughput. Adding bandwidth or changing network topology are two of the most likely solutions to severe network problems. The DBA should work closely with the system administrator to understand the operating system requirements of the SQL Server. You should also have a rudimentary understanding of basic performance overhead, and you should understand the fact that each component has its own particular role to play in the performance equation.

This book does not deal with network or hardware tuning in detail. You may find the article by Tim Quinlan called "How To Predict Client/Server Performance" to be a useful starting point. It elaborates a technique for factoring network overhead and other physical considerations into your own internal benchmarks. Sometimes this is useful. However, it is the author's opinion that most of the time these are peripheral issues. In our experience, it is usually something in the design rather than the hardware that is causing any given performance problem, and it is cheaper to create a good design up front than it is to throw money at a network.

If you are faced with a system crippled by poor performance, the following list acts as a useful starting point for a systematic approach to the problem. This book will enumerate these techniques in detail.

- Design. Good design techniques ensure the best possible performance for your system. Any database design must begin with the solid foundation of a conceptual model that is fully normalized to at least the third degree (3NF). Business Rules are a critical component of both the conceptual and logical data models. A complete understanding of business rules is required to achieve the best logical model, which includes considerations such as denormalization, overnormalization, and logical partitioning. Physical database design uses the logical model and transforms it into database structures customized to the database management system (in our case, Sybase) and the hardware configuration.

- Concurrency. As mentioned above, concurrency is a major, and usually neglected, component of overall system performance. The book discusses how to attack concurrency issues in the chapter on execution thread analysis.

- Parallelism. Parallel architectures in both hardware and operating systems are now widespread and relatively inexpensive. Databases are rising to the challenge, continually seeking to exploit this parallelism to achieve faster response time and throughput. By adding disks AND controllers (it is not enough to add disks; you must have multiple controllers), and by purchasing hardware platforms designed to accommodate multiple CPUs, you can take advantage of the benefits of parallelism. System XI has added several new DBA-tunable server parameters which improve the server's utilization of parallel CPUs.

- SQL Code. Writing efficient SQL code which exploits the optimizer's features is an obvious component of performance, but not the only component. Most developers focus on the SQL code at the expense of all the rest. In a situation that combines a bottleneck in concurrency, poor overall design, and improper server tuning, performance is going to be bad no matter how you tweak your queries. You should approach all performance problems with an open mind looking for a number of different solutions.

- Load Balancing. In some cases it is possible to off-load some processing to the client application, especially compute-intensive activities like math and aggregations. Databases are effective at storing data, not performing calculations. Use both the database and the client machine in your designs.

- Stored Procedures. Use stored procedures to download database processing such as cursors to the server. Remember that stored procedures are pre-parsed and pre-compiled, and almost always perform better than individual queries sent to the server.

- Macro tuning. This book discusses server tunable parameters in the context of each chapter as they are appropriate, but dedicates the last chapter to DBA-specific issues involving memory. It is often surprising how much a good DBA can enhance performance in a well-know environment. The database team needs to work together: DBA, designer, and developer—everyone doing their part to improve performance.

- Other client/server issues. Gateways cause particular problems, and there are many controversies about different middleware products such as ODBC. This book will not get involved in these controversies, but we do want to highlight an interesting aspect of tuning: Generic SQL. If you are going to submit the same query to several heterogeneous DBMSs, it helps to know how to make the query run well regardless of optimizer type. This book provides several insights in this area.

There are many ways to build performance throughout the development process. Several are listed here and expanded in the book:

- When gathering requirements, include information about performance estimates, expectations, and level of importance. State critical performance requirements as business rules and enforce them like any other business rule.

- Consider performance ramifications in both logical and physical database design. See the design chapter for more information.

- Consider access strategies and transaction design in advance for high-volume and/or high-usage tables. See the optimizer chapter for details.

- Write fast queries the first time, by understanding the optimizer.

- Design and configure the SQL Server with up-front knowledge of data volumetrics to minimize I/O and locks. See the chapter on locking for more information.
- Configure the overall client/server environment to minimize network I/O and balance CPU loads. Appropriately partition activities between the client and the server.
- Work with database gateways and write SQL code which performs well across all major optimizer types.
- For slow code that is already written, analyze the most wasteful transactions first.

1.3 Business Rules and Models

Business Rules are the heart of the enterprise. They represent the policies and rationale behind what the business does. Business rules are often neglected and not understood by the very people who should most concern themselves with them: the designers of enterprise-wide client/server applications.

A proper understanding of business rules is one of the most important ingredients in designing database applications, and it permeates every aspect of database design and development. The capture and enforcement of business rules is not just a requirement gathering exercise. If applications do not support the business rules, then they do not support the business.

Business rules control the performance tuning process. The designer must guarantee their enforcement, regardless of any tweaking done to enhance performance. This is especially important for transaction chopping. The thread analysis chapter outlines our methodology for transaction analysis, and business rules play a very prominent role.

In addition, there may be business rules which outline performance requirements. The relative importance of different activities of the business, as expressed in the business rules, dictates which transactions take precedence over others, and which should be optimized first when compromises must be made.

If you are unfamiliar with business rules and their effect on the database design and development process, here are several examples to help you understand their role (see Figure 1.4):

- "A student must be 15 years of age or older." This business rule represents a simple check, but helps to ensure that the birthday and acceptance date of each student in the database are correct relative to one another.
- "A student must have a department." This business rule represents a cross-table check and specifies what must happen in the database when a new student is added or when a department is deleted. All students under a deleted department must move to a new department, and the assignment process should be controlled by other business rules.
- "The attendance report must be submitted by 4:00 PM each business day." This business rule represents a regulation, but probably also specifies a performance requirement. If the data needed for the attendance report becomes available as the books update at 3:00 PM, and 400,000 transactions must be posted to create the attendance report, then this business rule gives the designer a performance requirement.

The importance of business rules will become clear as they are mentioned throughout the book.

Figure 1.4 and the tables below show the design of a simple college database, along with all of its business rules. This sample database is used in many of the examples throughout the rest of the book.

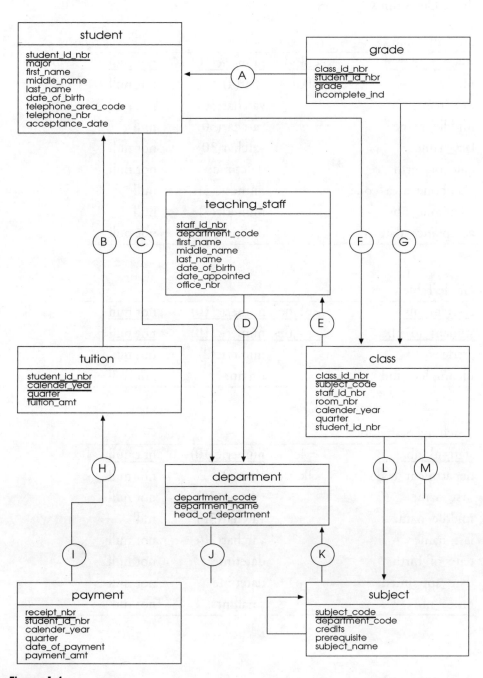

Figure 1.4
The College Database Example

Table Definitions:

Student Table

student_id_nbr	<pk>	numeric(10)	not null
major	<fk>	char(4)	not null
first_name		varchar(30)	not null
middle_name		varchar(30)	null
last_name		varchar(30)	not null
date_of_birth		datetime	not null
telephone_area_code		numeric(3)	null
telephone_nbr		numeric(7)	null
acceptance_date		datetime	not null

Grade Table

class_id_nbr	<pk,fk>	numeric(10)	not null
student_id_nbr	<pk,fk>	numeric(10)	not null
grade		numeric(2)	not null
incomplete_ind		tinyint	not null

Teaching_Staff Table

staff_id_nbr	<pk>	numeric(10)	not null
department_code	<fk>	char(4)	not null
first_name		varchar(30)	not null
middle_name		varchar(30)	null
last_name		varchar(30)	not null
date_of_birth		datetime	not null
date_appointed		datetime	not null
office_nbr		smallint	not null

Tuition Table

student_id_nbr	<pk,fk>	numeric(10)	not null
calender_year	<pk>	numeric(4)	not null
quarter	<pk>	char(6)	not null
tuition_amt		money	not null

Department Table

department_code	<pk>	char(4)	not null
department_name		varchar(30)	not null
head_of_department		varchar(30)	not null

Class Table

class_id_nbr	<pk>	numeric(10)	not null
subject_code	<fk>	char(7)	not null
staff_id_nbr	<fk>	numeric(10)	not null
room_nbr		smallint	not null
calender_year		numeric(4)	not null
quarter		char(6)	not null
student_id_nbr	<fk>	numeric(10)	not null

Payment Table

receipt_nbr	<pk>	numeric(10)	not null
student_id_nbr	<fk>	numeric(10)	not null
calender_year	<fk>	numeric(4)	not null
quarter	<fk>	char(6)	not null
date_of_payment		datetime	not null
payment_amt		money	not null

Subject Table

subject_code	<pk>	char(7)	not null
department_code	<fk>	char(4)	not null
credits		tinyint	not null
prerequisite	<fk>	char(7)	null
subject_name		varchar(30)	not null

Business Rules:

A   No grades can be issued before tuition is payed.

B   Each student must pay tuition.

C   A student must be assigned to at least one department.

D   Each teacher must belong to at least one department.

E   Each teacher must be qualified to teach an assigned class.

F   A student must take at least one class each quarter.

G   No grade can be granted before class is completed.

H   Payment in full is required before or on end of quarter.

I   Payment can not be divided into more than four payments total.

J   All sudents, teaching staff, and subjects must belong to at least one department.

K   All subjects must be assigned to at least one department.

L   Each class has zero or more qualifying prerequisite classes.

M   Each class must be assigned a room number.

1.4 Performance Metrics

A reactive designer measures database performance through user complaints. A proactive designer measures performance with benchmarks. Always design, create and test your own benchmarks as part of the general design and development process. Data demographics and skew influence performance in many different ways. You cannot improve what you cannot measure, and benchmarks give you the tools you need to measure performance. See Figure 1.5.

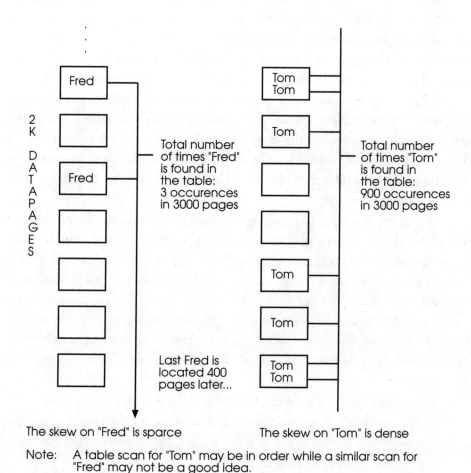

The skew on "Fred" is sparce   The skew on "Tom" is dense

Note: A table scan for "Tom" may be in order while a similar scan for
         "Fred" may not be a good idea.

Figure 1.5

Data Skew

SYSTEM XI

System XI provides a SET STATISTICS TIME utility which will report back the throughput of a command. Try out various strategies and record the time each command takes to execute. Don't forget load factors—run your tests during the peak times of the day, when many transactions are being sent to the server at once.

When using benchmarks, record your findings and keep historical records. Performance may degrade over time due to increased user load, table growth or hardware obsolescence, and the historical benchmarks may help to justify the purchase of new hardware or the redesign of certain parts of the database. Record time of day and user load when performing a benchmark.

When using benchmarks to improve performance, always verify that your "fix" really fixes a problem. Prove it with your benchmark numbers. Make sure you run test metrics against the same sort of data, and the same volume, in as close to a production environment as possible. You should test under the same conditions (number of users, system load, data demographics, etc.) as the production environment.

One of the best ways to obtain benchmark results prior to the production release, or to tune system performance after release, is to use a "sandbox." A sandbox is so named because it lets you "play" with the database without causing harm or production shutdowns. A sandbox recreates the production environment's data and traffic in a laboratory setting, allowing you to test and verify tuning and design strategies without affecting users of the production system. Prior to the production release, a sandbox contains either simulated or historic data and will give you your only accurate model against which you can test your designs.

A good sandbox will have the following characteristics and features:

- The sandbox's server machine will have the same characteristics as the production server. It will use the same CPU, memory configuration, disks and controller architecture.
- The data in the database will have the same demographics, skew and volume as production data.
- The system should experience user loading similar to that which it will see in the production environment. Several different products available on the market today make it relatively easy to simulate user load. You can use network debugging tools to simulate other network traffic. Make sure that user loading during peak times is also simulated. For example, if your database will see its highest load at week's end, year's end, Christmas, etc., make sure you simulate these situations.

Given a sandbox this accurate, it is extremely easy to gather benchmark results and try different tactics to improve system performance. During the latter parts of the design process a sandbox can help determine the actual implementation of the physical design. Once the system is in production, the sandbox acts as an experimental database that you can use to create and verify hypotheses.

1.5 Troubleshooting

After-the-fact performance tuning is called *troubleshooting*. When troubleshooting, you are Sherlock Holmes ferreting out the elusive, hidden problem by following clues.

Jim and Mary Panttaja, in an insightful talk at the International Sybase User Conference in 1995, provided a list of helpful "Sleuthing Steps" which can aid you in your quest for meaning from the clues. Ask these questions:

1. What is "The Problem"? Ask users to specifically describe and demonstrate the performance problem they are experiencing.

2. What is the Environment? Examine and document the hardware and software environment.

3. Is the problem most likely at the client or the server?

4. What does the database really look like? Do not use ERDs, as they could be out of synch with the actual database.

5. What do the indexes look like?

6. What do the transactions look like?

7. Is there blocking? Check the error logs and use server statistics to find out.

8. How do your client and server tools interact? See Figure 1.6.

They recommend looking at the symptoms of the problem and narrowing things down as best you can, first to client or server (or sometimes both). Then narrow the problem down further until you discover what you think is the main source of difficulty. Create hypotheses, design solution strategies, and test them. Prove that the results are indeed corrective, then implement the results in the production environment—the ultimate test.

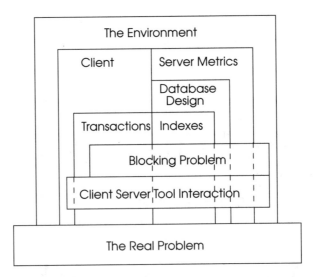

Figure 1.6

Interrelated aspects of troubleshooting techniques. For example, blocking problems should be analyzed in the light of transactions, indexes, database design, server metrics, and the overall environment.

In some cases a benchmark may show improvement and you may think you've found the source of the problem. After some period of time, the problem may reassert itself. In these cases, it is likely you did not uncover the real problem. Start over and reevaluate the symptoms of the problem from the beginning.

1.6 Elements of the Performance Problem

In a huge database system, it is easy to become overwhelmed by the complexity and scope of performance problems. Component interaction can lead to situations that seem nearly impossible to understand. In these situations it is best to recall that a database, no matter how large and complex, consists of a collection of extremely simple elements that behave in known ways.

Imagine that you want to store data electronically. At present you have just one option: disk drives. Current drive technology divides the total space available on the drive into fixed-size sectors. To read or write a sector requires between one and 10 milliseconds on most modern drives. For the sake of the examples here let's use five milliseconds as the average read and write time for any sector.

Sybase uses these sectors to create fixed size pages of 2K bytes each. You store your data on one or more of these pages. In a relational database data typically exists on a page in a fixed-size row that contains a number of fields or columns. The size of a row determines the number of rows that can fit on a page.

Imagine that you want to store the name, address and phone number of your clients on a disk drive. Your data might consume 200 bytes per client, for a total of 10 rows per page. If you have 100,000 clients your database will require 10,000 pages collected together in a table. The system will keep track of the first and last page, and it will create pointers on each page that link the 10,000 pages together.

The only easy way to add data to your database is to place new rows at the end of the table. Therefore the data resides in the table in a random order. If you want to find anything in the table you must perform a table scan starting at the beginning of the table. To scan 10,000 pages will require 50,000 milliseconds, or 50 seconds. Obviously this sort of delay is unacceptable. Therefore all DBMSs allow you to add one or more indexes to a table. An index, like an index for a book, lets you jump to an appropriate point in the table to find the data you need immediately. Indexes can be clustered or non-clustered. A table can have one clustered index and as many non-clustered indexes as you like. If a table has a clustered index, the data is stored in the table in sorted order according to the order established by the clustered index. Non-clustered indexes simply point into the data in the table in its existing order.

An index duplicates the search key data in a B-Tree structure. Therefore, an index consumes disk space in relation to the size of the keys it contains. An index also lives on disk, so it takes time relative to the tree depth to find a specific row's location in the table. It might take between three and ten disk accesses to trace through the branches of an index and find a specific record. While this is a dramatic improvement over the 10,000 disk accesses required for a table scan, it still consumes up to 50 milliseconds and means that you can perform at most 20 to 100 index searches per second in the absence of caching.

Also note that indexes slow insertion, update and delete times. When you add something to a table that has no indexes (known as a heap table), the new row lands on the last page of the table in one disk access. When the table has one or more non-clustered indexes, the data still lands on the last page of the table but the system must update all indexes well. In a table with a clustered index, the new row lands on the appropriate page to maintain sorted order. If this page is full, the database must split the page and copy and delete appropriate rows across the two pages. All of these activities, especially on a heavily indexed table, take time. You can therefore see that indexes are both good and bad. They can significantly improve query speed and you want to use them heavily on query intensive tables, but they hurt insertion and update performance so you want to use them sparingly. This dichotomy leads to two different types of systems:

- Decision Support Systems (DSSs), where the emphasis is on looking things up in the database to help the decision making process. In a DSS the data is largely read-only and is heavily indexed.
- On-Line Transaction Processing systems (OLTP), where the emphasis is on inserting and updating the data. Table modification is heavy in these systems and therefore extra indexes are to be avoided.

Because disk access is so slow, there is always a desire to speed up disk access. One way to do so is to cache frequently or recently used information from the disk in memory in the hope that it will be used again. Data retrieved from cache arrives 100 to 1,000 times more quickly than data retrieved from disk, providing a significant performance boost. If you can afford it, one of the easiest ways to solve many performance problems is to provide the server machine with enough memory to cache the entire database. This is not uncommon on mission critical databases containing less than 200 megabytes of data.

The discussion so far has assumed a single user. When multiple users access the same database the system must manage certain concurrency issues. For example, if one process is trying to write to a page, it needs to have exclusive access to the page during the entire write operation. This exclusivity is managed with a lock. During the write operation, the lock keeps any other readers or writers away from the page until the write completes. A user who wants to access a locked page therefore waits. If one user wants to write to a page that 100 users want to read, all 100 readers will have to wait until the write completes. This contention for specific pages can become severe if not managed properly. Keep in mind also that a heavily used system can have hundreds or thousands of locks in place at any given moment. Locks consume space and take time.

To keep track of all the pages in a table, the size of the table, the indexes pointing to the table and so on, the system maintains its own information in system tables. Many operations require updates to the system tables, and all of these updates can consume fairly significant amounts of time because they require disk access. The system also manages a temporary area called tempdb as well as a set of log files. Tempdb handles operations like sorting, where data in a record set is copied to a new temporary table to perform the sort operation. The log file keeps track of database activity and state. Because the system uses these two facilities heavily they are two of the best things to optimize, either by placing them on their own drives or by caching them heavily.

The server's job is to execute SQL code to retrieve or modify the data in the tables. As the complexity of the database rises through the addition of tables and indexes, the server's job gets harder. For example, on any given select statement the server has to decide whether or not to use an index and which index is most appropriate for the query. The optimizer is in charge of making these decisions. If the optimizer makes bad decisions, however, the performance of your system can fall rapidly. It is therefore important to overall system performance to make sure the optimizer is behaving as expected, or to add or modify indexes and queries to make the optimizer perform as expected.

From this discussion, you can see that many, if not most, of the features of a modern DBMS exist for the express purpose of improving performance. Indexes, caches and the optimizer do nothing but boost the speed of database activities. You can also see that, when you have a performance problem, there are a finite number of tools available to solve the problem. You can:

- Add, delete or modify indexes
- Add cache memory or use it in better ways
- Improve your queries
- Improve the way the optimizer handles your queries
- Manage contention
- Reduce the size of tables

The goal of this book is to help you to understand these mechanisms and the ways in which you can use them to improve performance of new or existing systems.

As an example of how the different constraints imposed by the different components described above can interact, Figure 1.7 shows a database diagram

for a large client/server database handling OLTP, DSS and EDI transaction responsibilities. In this figure the emphasis is on the interaction of the three main
components of the system when an EDI transaction arrives.

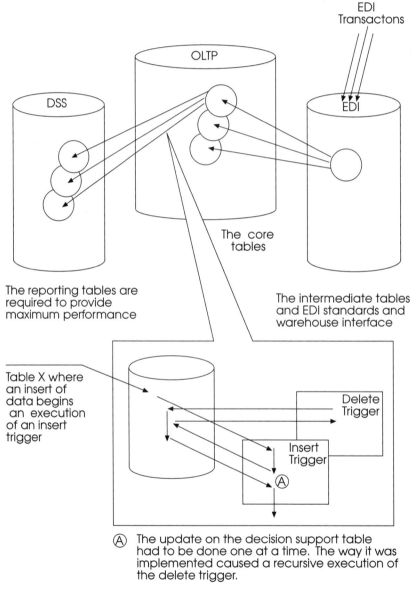

Figure 1.7
A Typical Client/Server Database Design

This design had evolved over the course of four years as the database grew in size and scope. The OLTP portion of the database acts as the core, accepting data from between 30 and 100 simultaneous users. Initially the OLTP code was the entire database, with DSS activities such as ad hoc queries and reporting using the OLTP tables directly. As time passed, the reporting activity became more and more burdensome and required more and more indexes, which hurt OLTP performance. The DSS portion was therefore split off into a separate set of heavily indexed tables (seven to 10 indexes per table), allowing the OLTP portion of the database to reduce its index load to an average of three indexes per table.

EDI transactions also initially arrived at the OLTP core. A separate EDI area in the database was created for two reasons. First, it allowed EDI transaction verification testing and cleanup to occur in a "safe" area before moving the data into the OLTP area. Second it allowed load balancing. The EDI transactions could queue up in the EDI section and release at times of low load on the OLTP section.

The diagram shows the release process for an EDI transaction. Each transaction modified approximately 25 tables in the OLTP section of the database, with an additional 75 indexes for those tables needing updates as well. Then 12 tables and approximately 100 indexes would require updates in the DSS section. This level of activity required about three minutes for each EDI transaction. Tuning was able to reduce that time to two minutes.

The question: What do you do when the average number of EDI transactions per hour rises above 30? There are several options:

- Tune further
- Delay updates to the DSS tables to once per hour or once per day if acceptable
- Add CPU power to the server
- Add cache memory

The ultimate solution was to use all of the different techniques described in this book until no further improvements could be found, and then move to a new architecture shown in Figure 1.8. In this approach, there is a total separation between the OLTP and DSS portions of the database. They run on completely separate machines. A replication server keeps the two databases in sync.

This approach works well whenever you have largely independent areas in a database.

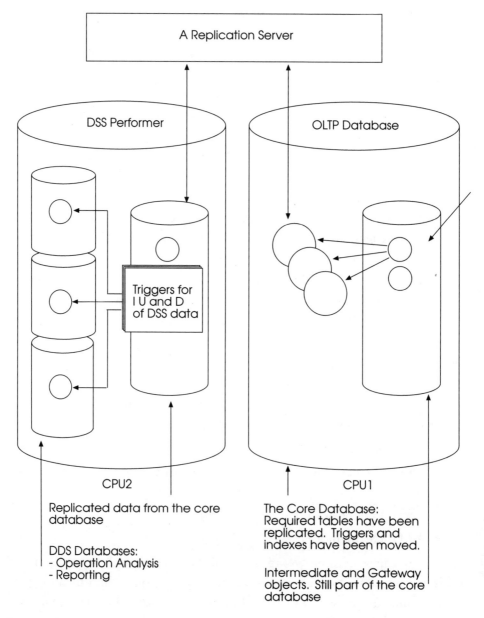

Figure 1.8

The New Design Using a Replication Server

1.7 Summary: Dos and Don'ts

- DO consider that application performance is based upon many factors.
- DO spend your time analyzing the "best bang for your buck" situations. Focus on transactions consuming the most resources.
- DO embed performance strategies into every phase of the software development lifecycle.
- DO build performance considerations into both logical and physical designs.
- DO remember to look at the overall client/server environment for performance issues.
- DON'T forget to consider the "Big Picture": server issues.
- DON'T concentrate so much on individual query speed that you neglect design factors.
- DON'T neglect locking considerations in transaction design.

Design

2

The design of an application's database creates the basic structure through which all queries access data. The design of the database is therefore central to the fundamental performance of any client/server system. A good design is the fundamental foundation upon which you build applications able to support many users concurrently. Similarly, a poor design gives you very little chance of producing good performance, especially in a multi-user environment. Poor designs force premature re-engineering and are therefore extremely expensive in both a financial and spiritual sense. See Figure 2.1.

There are several different measures of "goodness" in the design of a multi-user client/server database, and it is the job of the designer to choose among these measures as specified in the business rules and as appropriate. For example, you might measure a design by its purity in terms of normalization. While this measure has a number of advantages, it often leads to poor performance. Therefore, you might choose to measure the goodness of your design by its performance. Performance generally leads to compromise, however. The cost of performance is often more difficult maintenance and unexpected side-effects. In addition, a database design driven solely by performance can quickly become so confusing that it is impossible to understand. As the designer you must find a way to balance the different measures.

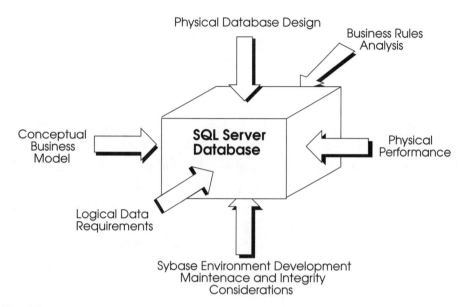

Figure 2.1
Significant Database Influences

In this chapter you will learn about different options available in the design of a database that allow you to choose your performance compromises carefully. The three-phase design methodology, when used appropriately, gives you the opportunity to choose different measures at different points in the design. You can therefore concentrate on a particular measure without worrying about its cost or side-effects.

2.1 The Phases of Design

Data modeling consists of the development of the Conceptual Data Model, the Logical Data Model, and the Physical Data Model. It is the Physical Data Model that you use to produce the actual database schema.

2.2 The Conceptual Data Model

The conceptual data model consists of entity sets framed in subject areas. For example, if you are developing a database application that holds financial and accounting information, most of the entities in the conceptual data model are associated with finance. Entities in such a database might include a general ledger table set, accounts receivable, accounts payable, etc.

The entities should exist in at least third normal form in the conceptual model. The state of normalization is extremely important when considering a starting point for performance tuning. In the latter stages of development you may find a part of the database that is not working as expected, so it is sometimes necessary to revert back to the original normalized model and trace the steps taken to arrive at the physical representation for the data. Without a normalized model to act as a starting point, it is often impossible to understand the intent of tactics used to improve performance, and the database becomes unmaintainable. At times, performance tuning necessitates iterative redesign, where you cycle between the Conceptual, Logical and Physical Data Models searching for the best performance possible. Normalization in the conceptual data model produces the most resilient, flexible structure for this sort of iteration.

It is possible to directly implement the Conceptual Model as your physical database schema, but generally this approach is successful only when working on very small databases. Hardware and software are not able to support a large scale conceptual model. We are bound by I/O, network bandwidth and CPU speed from implementing the true relational model that Ted Codd developed, as discussed in the next section.

Normalization, a vital component of the conceptual model, is beyond the scope of this book. We recommend books by either C. J. Date or Barbara von Halle for more information on this topic. See the bibliography for further information on these books.

2.3 The Logical Model

Business rules gradually become integrated into the conceptual model, and they transform it into the Logical Model. The business rules set performance standards based on the priorities of the business and guide performance tuning. They add essential business knowledge to the task of performance tuning. For example, if you tune something that is not highly relevant to the business, your work will not provide value. Business rules bring development into proper perspective.

The following sections suggest performance tuning options available to a designer working at the level of the logical model.

2.3.1   Denormalization

Business rules play an essential role in making performance-oriented changes in the Logical Model. To demonstrate the effect of business rules, imagine a typical student database that you might find at the registrar's office of a college. See Section 1.3. A database designer would, at some point during the analysis process for the database, define the concept of the "Grade Point Average," or GPA, of a student. The GPA is the current running average of the grades for a given student. It includes all classes completed and does not include all classes currently being taken. This definition of a GPA is a business rule. Other business rules indicate how to handle special cases such as incomplete classes, classes taken for credit only, and so on. Many other business rules in the system involve GPA. For example, the definition of the concept of an honor roll, the definition of probation, graduation criteria, and so on, all depend on the GPA. Because of the importance of the GPA concept, the designer may decide that the logical model would serve the business better if each student record in the student table contained a special GPA field.

Adding a GPA field is a violation of normalization because the GPA of a student is a derived fact. However, because it is accessed so often and represents a vital piece of information to the college, it is placed in the student table as a separate field. The performance advantage results from not having to recalculate the GPA for a student every time it is needed. For this approach to work, the GPA field must remain current. The database must recalculate the GPA when any new grades are added or existing grades are changed. This synchronization of the GPA field with the rest of the database will mean that updates are slower. In addition, the logical model now must incorporate certain new business rules into its design to force synchronization. These synchronization rules control the accuracy of derived data. The logical model needs to be fully documented, and the documentation should contain the design rationale, any necessary maintenance, and tests that can later verify the accuracy of the derived field.

Although this is an extremely simple example, it demonstrates how easy it is for denormalization to creep into a database for performance reasons. It is almost required. No database could support the effort of recalculating a student's GPA from scratch each time it is needed. In a large database the number of simple modifications like this one can become enormous, and they must be managed carefully.

Denormalization often reduces the total number of entities in the design. The process of denormalization may involve combining two tables or collapsing associative (intersect) entities. For example, you might include a name field from a detail table into the master table and thereby avoid a join with the detail table. If the detail table contains a name and a code, you can sometimes completely eliminate the need for the table. For example a student's major, indicated in the student table as a join to the department_code in the department table, can be stored in a field of the student table. If reports are continually produced which reference the department name, it will avoid the overhead of a join to include the department name in the student table. Once again, you will need to add business rules enforcing update integrity. If a department changes its name, the new name must propagate to the student table. This sort of activity is classified as denormalization because the department name field depends upon the major field, and has no direct dependency upon the primary key.

An interesting kind of denormalization can occur with associative entities. You can sometimes eliminate a join by including the pertinent field(s) in the associative table. For instance, if an application frequently generates student grade lists and this operation requires fast response time, try including the first and last names of the student in the grade table. Since all of the relevant information appears in one table you can eliminate the join with the student table.

There is nothing wrong with this sort of performance-related tuning, except that it makes maintenance harder later on. Each modification made to the conceptual model requires extra documentation and testing.

2.3.2   Overnormalization

It can be advantageous to break very large tables into smaller tables for performance reasons, a process known as overnormalization. The process of denormalization often results in fewer tables, while overnormalization results in more tables. The sheer size of some tables limits performance, especially when the information in the table is not equally pertinent to all users.

Overnormalization is based on two relatively simple types of fragmentation. See Figure 2.2. There are multiple reasons for overnormalization: Overnormalization by size, function and date are all common. You can also normalize by utilization. If a table includes some information that is not used as heavily as the rest of information in the table, you can separate out the less-used columns into their own table. This technique works especially well if the underused data is bulky. For instance, comment fields tend to be large (255 characters) and infrequently used. You can often obtain a performance benefit by placing comments in their own table. Text and image data can reside in their own tables as well.

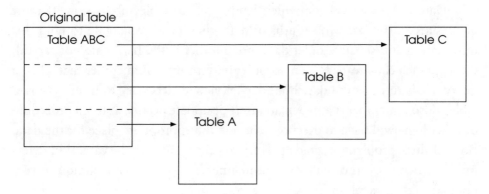

Overnormalization: Horizontal Fragmentation

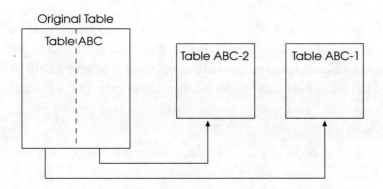

Overnormalization: Vertical Fragmentation

Figure 2.2
Two Basic Types of Fragmentation

You can also overnormalize by function. For example, in a college database there may be student information used only by the Bursar's office. Scholarship eligibility codes, in-state tuition codes, tuition rate codes, and so on are important to the Bursar but not to the Registrar. Even though this information may directly relate to the student id on a one-to-one basis, and therefore belongs in the student table, you can separate it into its own table. Since many different departments and users query the student table, and only the financial department cares about these fields, performance will improve for non-financial users. To recover the performance lost in the Bursar's office, you can denormalize some of the student fields into the student financial table to eliminate the required join.

Date is another criteria which lends itself to table subdivision. If most queries access the last two months of data, then create one table to hold this information and separate older data into another table. If you are not careful, this approach can create as many problems as it solves. Remember that when a query needs to cross the date boundary, a view is necessary to union the two tables. Also remember that when an insert or update occurs, a stored procedure or other logic will have to execute to decide the appropriate place for the data. Both of these problems degrade performance, so you must be careful in determining when to overnormalize in this manner. This particular technique is very popular in data warehousing.

2.3.3   Using Derived Data for Referential Integrity

If a derived summary field exists in a master table, you can often avoid an access to a detail table to check referential integrity. You can use this technique if you are using triggers for referential integrity checks and you have a derived field, like GPA or a sum, in the master table. Because a zero value in the derived column indicates no detail rows, you can avoid an access to the detail table for an existence check.

Here is a common example: In a college database, imagine a business rule that says, "do not delete a Tuition Bill if it has associated Line Items." This rule specifies a referential integrity check. Instead of accessing the Line Item table to determine if line items exist, you can instead check the value of Total Tuition in the Tuition Bill table. If this field is zero, you can assume that there are no associated line items.

tuition			
student_id_nbr	<pk,fk>	numeric(10)	not null
calender_year	<pk>	numeric(4)	not null
quarter	<pk>	char(6)	not null
tuition_amt		money	not null

Figure 2.3
Tuition Table

If you think about this technique carefully, you can see that you must use caution. You have to check other business rules carefully, and in certain cases add new business rules, to make it work properly. For example, you must verify that a zero tuition bill does not have special meaning in the environment. You must also create a business rule that states that line items with a zero amount are illegal. Consider the case of a person who has had his or her tuition waived and therefore has a zero bill even though several line items might exist separately.

You might also use different signaling mechanisms to indicate that there are no line items in the database. For example, you can use a "-1" for some of these cases, or you make the Total Tuition field nullable and specify in a business rule that a null value indicates no line items. All of these approaches are compromises however, and will get messy as the database grows. Probably a better approach is to create a separate derived field that indicates the number of line items that exist in the Line Item table. Then you can check this field to decide whether or not line items exist.

2.3.4   "Mini-Warehouse": Another Way to Overnormalize

If you have too much contention between inserts/updates and queries, you might consider an approach called "mini-warehousing." This technique involves cloning the functionality of a table or group of tables. The clone is marked read-mostly and is used for decision support (queries only), while the original is used OLTP (insert and updates). You can keep the read-only tables synchronized with the OLTP tables by using triggers, stored procedures or a replication server. The beauty of this strategy is that queries never contend with write operations and users therefore do not have to wait for exclusive locks. By removing the contention, the performance boost can be dramatic.

You need to carefully evaluate your load strategy when using this technique. You must precisely determine how often your DSS (Decision Support System) table gets refreshed. Triggers may cause just as much contention as a direct write, because they occur at the same time (in real time) and they also require an exclusive lock. If users can live with aged data, then you can avoid this sort of contention by using periodic rather than immediate synchronization. Refreshing the read-only tables every night, during a low-load period, lets you balance your load across the day and works well if users can work with day-old data.

You can easily see from the above examples that any modifications made to the logical model in the name of performance involve a compromise. Performance-related modifications to the conceptual model inevitably complicate things, add business rules, make maintenance harder and often create performance side-effects somewhere else in the system. You must therefore chose and document your modifications carefully. On the other hand, you can also see that it will be much easier to make performance-related decisions like those described above in the design phase. Trying to graft them into a production system is disruptive and much more time-consuming, especially when tables have grown large.

2.3.4.1   The Physical Model

The logical model incorporates business rules into the Conceptual Data Model, and often adds new business rules to make sure that the compromises and modifications chosen for the logical model do not corrupt the data. Once this process is complete you are ready to design the physical model. The physical model takes advantage of all the important performance features that Sybase offers. These features include clustered indexes, constraints, rules, etc.

The designer uses the physical model to take advantage of special features offered by a particular database engine or hardware environment, or to create workarounds to avoid any known deficiencies. The physical model melds hardware architecture, DBMS architecture and application logic together into a tuned unit. For example, in an SMP hardware architecture you design the number and structure of indexes differently than you would in a single CPU environment. If multiple CPUs are simultaneously accessing a single table with many indexes, it results in much lower performance than it would if the table had only one or two indexes. You therefore use this particular piece of knowledge in your physical model.

How might you gain this particular piece of knowledge, and how do you determine its validity in your particular environment? This is an important question in any performance tuning exercise: you must know the strengths and constraints of the hardware environment. You will often use a prototype or proof-of-concept model to determine how your hardware behaves in certain situations. A model may be the only way to get a true sense of how all of the different forces in your system will interact. A good sandbox, as described in Chapter 1, is essential to creating a good physical design.

In the sections below we discuss several issues that you should consider in physical design: Row size, nullable columns, physical table structure and disk placement, and index design. The latter is an essential part of any physical design, and it is covered in more depth in the index chapter of this book.

2.3.5 Row Size

Row size can affect performance in several different ways. Generally, the larger the row size, the slower the query. This phenomena occurs because rows physically live in fixed-size pages on disk. Large rows require more pages, which lead the database engine to perform more disk accesses. Row size decisions therefore involve a balancing act between two conflicting goals:

- Rows frequently accessed together should exist on the same page to minimize I/O. This rule, called co-residency, implies that you should put as many rows as possible on a page to minimize the number of pages read.
- However, the more rows per page, the higher the likelihood that two or more users will need the same page at the same time. This situation leads to contention. To avoid contention, you want to lower the density of rows per page.

Sybase uses page level locking instead of row level locking, and this is another important concern. See the chapter on locks for more information.

For any given database or table, the optimum case lies somewhere between the extremes of one row on a page (which is a ridiculous waste of space) and a large number of rows per page. John Kirkwood proposes that optimum row size is about 10-20% of page size (see the bibliography for more informa-

tion about his books). Since page size is 2K bytes in Sybase, Kirkwood's pro-
posal means that the optimum row size is about 200 to 400 bytes. According
to Kirkwood, this number achieves a balance between page/row density and co-
residency concerns.

The above rules relate to queries. There are other concerns when you consider insertions. Tables that accept inserts in real time should have a fillfactor
that leaves at least one empty row per page to handle inserts. See Figure 2.4.
This fillfactor allows the database engine to add rows to pages without forcing
a page split on every insert. To determine the fillfactor you must know your row
size. See the locking chapter for additional information about fillfactor and
rows_per_page.

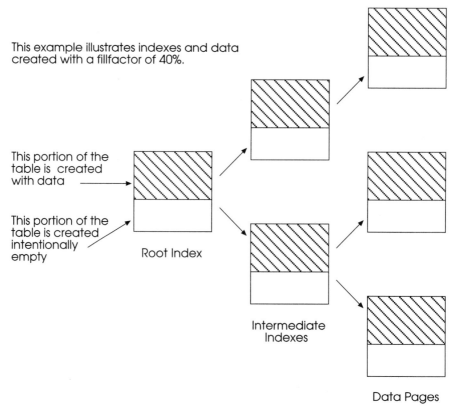

This example illustrates indexes and data
created with a fillfactor of 40%.

This portion of the
table is created
with data

This portion of the
table is created
intentionally
empty

Root Index

Intermediate
Indexes

Data Pages

Figure 2.4
Fill Factor

> **WARNING**
> Fillfactor is a performance booster for tables where heavy inserts are ex-
> pected. It is used only at the creation of the index. The reason for this is
> that constant maintenance would be no different than a full table with no
> fillfactor because it would be splitting the table at the same position every
> time.

If you find that several tables have rows with a size significantly greater
than 200 to 400 bytes, consider moving either specialized function fields or infrequently accessed columns to a different table, as discussed in the overnormalization section above. In any case, you should never allow a row to take up
more than half a page, because the wasted disk space causes table scans to take
twice as long.

The only exception to this rule would be the case where you are purposefully forcing a table to place one row per page to compensate for concurrency
problems caused by Sybase's page-level locking mechanism. In this case, you
might purposefully add dummy columns to consume enough space to force
each row onto a separate page. Sybase System XI provides a new way to accomplish the same thing: max_rows_per_page can be specified to limit the number
of rows that can fit on a page. The trade-offs, of course, are space and time. You
are trading disk space for access time to solve a concurrency problem. On large
tables this approach is obviously unworkable.

If your rows are too short you will get too many per page. High-density
pages often cause concurrency and locking problems. For pre-System XI releases, use a filler column to achieve row sizes between 200 and 400 bytes. For System XI, use max_rows_per_page, and specify a value between five and 10.

2.3.6   NULLable Columns in Sybase

Columns that allow NULL values have the potential of causing both major and subtle performance problems. A clear understanding of the effects of
nullable fields leads to better physical designs.

NULLable columns in Sybase are treated in the same manner as variable
length columns. They therefore have extra processing overhead, and more importantly forbid in-place updates. If the server cannot perform an update in

place, it will perform a delete and an insert during the update. The inserted row will usually be positioned elsewhere in the table, leaving a blank row in the middle of the data page. The resulting fragmentation causes page sparseness, leading to excessive I/O, and also wastes space.

If you have a column in which you are considering allowing NULLs, analyze how often you will need to update the column. If you expect frequent updates, consider a creative approach to the NULLABILITY issue. If the column is a character field, consider using a value like "n/a" or "not available" instead of NULL. If it is an integer, consider using -1 (if -1 does not already have meaning for that field). If it is a date, consider using "1/1/1900".

NULLable columns included in an index, either clustered or nonclustered, slow things down because of processing overhead. Try not to include them or variable length fields in any of your indexes.

2.3.7   Physical Table Placement

The way you implement the transaction log in your physical design can lead to significant performance gains. This surprising result occurs because the transaction log is a central part of the Sybase recovery mechanism and is therefore accessed almost constantly. The authors have had tremendous success with putting a high activity transaction log on a solid state device. Obviously this approach is expensive because the device itself is expensive and it must be backed up with battery power. Remember that without the transaction log recovery is impossible, and treat the log with the respect it therefore deserves. If a memory device is too expensive or risky in your environment, you should create a named cache for the log as well as several I/O pools. See Figure 2.5.

You should separate large, highly used tables and put each on its own device. By doing this you avoid disk contention between tables. You can also separate nonclustered indexes for these tables and put them on a device separate from their table. You can split up a large table by assigning additional segments to it, thereby spreading it out over more than one device. This method does not allow automatic balancing across the segments, but in many cases that problem will be irrelevant or manageable.

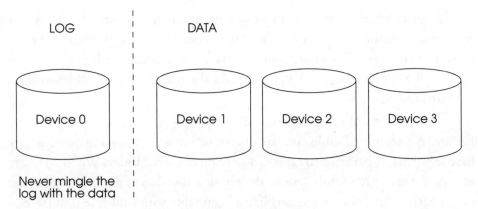

Warning: If you consider using a solid state device for Device 0 it must be
          backed up by battery and steps must be taken to make sure it
          never fills.

Figure 2.5
Physical Data Placement

WARNING

If you consider using a solid state device for Device 0 it must be backed
up by battery and steps must be taken to make sure it never fills up.

When you use separate devices for large tables or Sybase segments, each
device should operate using a dedicated controllers. Many disk hardware architectures that share the same controller with multiple devices cause the devices
to contend with each other for controller use. This effect negates any performance gain. Make sure that you configure your hardware properly and install
additional disk controllers if necessary.

SYSTEM XI

Configure a named cache for heavily accessed tables so they will not need
to compete with other tables for space in the cache. If a part of your design
requires numerous sequential page reads, increase the I/O size by creating
an I/O pool in the named cache for the table. See the Memory chapter for
more details.

2.3.8   Using Sybase System XI's Table Partitions

High-volume tables that must accept frequent concurrent inserts can cause major performance bottlenecks if they have a clustered index on a monotonic primary key. This contention occurs because Sybase will place all new rows on the last data page. This phenomena also occurs on heap tables with no clustered index.

One solution to this problem is to use System XI's new table partitioning feature. A partitioned table consists of two or more partitions mapped to Sybase segments. A partitioned table can have no clustered index. When an insert occurs, the server randomly assigns the physical location of the new row to one of the partitions. This scheme acts like a heap table with multiple "last pages," where the number of "last pages" is controlled by the number of partitions. All inserts still go to the "last page," but they are spread out evenly over the partitions. See Figure 2.6.

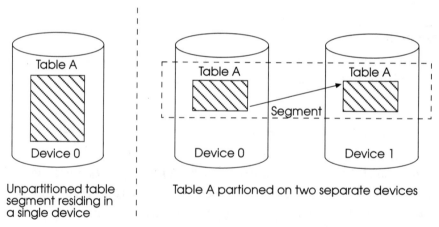

Unpartitioned table segment residing in a single device

Table A partioned on two separate devices

Note: With the data partitioned over multiple devices the probability that simulatneous data access will occur increases.

Figure 2.6
Physical Table Partioning

There is a trade-off that you must consider before committing to this scheme. You lose the performance gain obtained with a clustered index, since the partitioned table by definition cannot have a clustered index. You must examine how the table is used in your design to understand whether the approach has value. See the indexing chapter for more information about this monotonic key problem.

2.3.9 Index Design

Every table should have at least one index. The only possible exception to this rule is a very small table which can completely fit into memory. Tables that consume just one or two disk pages fit this description. On tiny tables like these, no benefit is gained from the index but the overhead of the index slows inserts because Sybase must update both the index and the data.

Any other table should have an index because the lack of an index forces the optimizer to choose a table scan. Without an index there is no way to know when all records have been found. For instance, an ordinary select statement finding just one row will still cause a table scan because it does not know when to stop looking:

```
Select LNAME from Student where SID = 432179
```

Unless there is an index on the SID column, this SELECT statement will cause a table scan. Unique indexes are important because they tell the optimizer to look for one and only one value. See Figure 2.6.

2.3.10 Clustered Index

Most tables should have a clustered index. A clustered index forces the data to be stored on the physical device in the same order as that specified by the index. This arrangement improves performance during sequential access. Clustered indexes should be used on join fields (usually the primary key), or frequently used search fields. Clustered indexes are also effective for range searches, which request a consecutive set of values.

Monotonic keys present a special challenge to clustered indexes and inserts. The previous section on table layout and partitioning illustrated one solution to this problem. See the chapter on Indexes for some other ideas. See Figure 2.7.

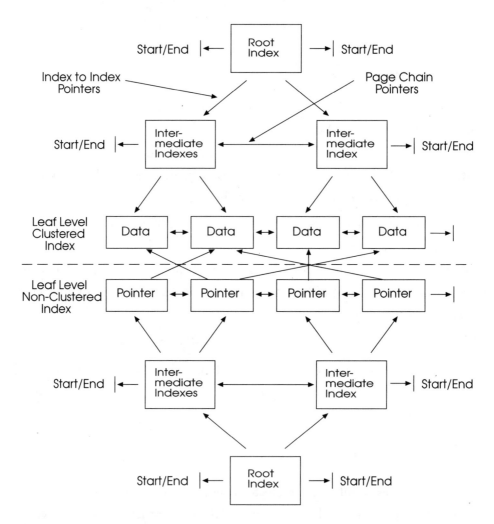

Note: The major difference between clustered and non-clustered indexes is that the clustered index ends with data at the leaf level while the non-clustered index ends with a pointer to the data.

Figure 2.7
Index Structure

2.3.11   Nonclustered Indexes

Nonclustered indexes offer significant performance increases, especially for single row results. They are excellent for "covering" a query: When all the fields specified in the SELECT clause are used in a nonclustered index, the optimizer does not have to access the data page, because all the needed information is contained in the leaf index page. You save one level of I/O in this situation.

Avoid creating too many nonclustered indexes for any individual table unless the table is a DSS table used in a read-mostly mode. Excessive indexing will slow down all insert, update and delete operations because all index structures must be kept up to date. You must take care to balance query speed with insertion speed depending on the usage pattern that you expect for the table.

2.4 Summary: Dos and Don'ts

- DO start with a normalized conceptual model before you begin tuning for performance.

- DO use denormalization and overnormalization to tune the logical model for performance.

- DO consider row size for highly accessed tables, and try to have between four to 10 rows per page.

- DO NOT use NULLable fields if you can avoid them. They cause several different kinds of performance degradation in Sybase, and they require more overhead than NOT NULL columns.

- DO separate the transaction log from the rest of your data and put it on a separate disk.

- DO use segments to spread out high usage tables across different disks.

- DO use table partitions to avoid last page "hot spots" in heap tables.

- DO have a clustered index on every table, except small ones.

- DO use nonclustered indexes to cover some queries.

UNDERSTANDING THE OPTIMIZER

3

The optimizer provides Sybase with an automated way to enhance database performance. Because it is automated, however, you must understand how the optimizer works in order to write effective queries. The purpose of this chapter is to present insights into the inner-workings of the Sybase optimizer. We will emphasize the following:

- Understanding the optimizer from a practitioner's point of view
- Understanding how the optimizer works with indexes
- Understanding the most important optimizer components and nuances
- Using Showplan to analyze optimizer output
- Using DBCC TRACEON(3604, 302) to analyze how the optimizer made its decisions

3.1 The Optimizer

The primary objective of the optimizer is to provide the fastest possible physical access to data. There are different types of optimizers, the most common being cost-based and rule-based. Sybase System XI's optimizer is a cost-based optimizer. This book focuses entirely on the Sybase cost-based optimizer.

The optimizer is an integral component of the Sybase Server's engine. It compiles a query plan that the Sybase engine will immediately execute. The optimizer develops its query plan using statistics on index key distribution, row density, cache type, cache size, and I/O size. Several distinct improvements enhance the Sybase optimizer in the System XI release. For example, computations are now done in double precision as opposed to single-precision as in System 10.

The Sybase optimizer is robust and powerful and continues to evolve to solve performance problems in large scale client/server systems. It is interesting to note that as the various DBMS vendors have positioned themselves to take advantage of different portions of the database marketplace, the specific optimizers have been tailored to accommodate the general strategic goal or philosophy of that specific vendor. For example some vendors favor OLTP throughput as opposed to first record response time in their optimizer, and you can learn a great deal about a vendor's priorities by understanding these differences.

3.2 Cost-Based vs. Rule Based Optimizers

The rule-based optimizer used by Oracle version 6 and below determines access strategy by using a preprogramed set of access rules. This type of optimizer requires that the rules be established and interrogated. The major weakness of this approach is that the rules are not variable and cannot account for changing table sizes or the physical location of indexes. Equally limiting is the fact that you cannot tune rule-based optimizers to handle growth and or increasing access frequency and volume.

In contrast, a cost-based optimizer uses variably changing statistics on the database objects to develop its access strategy. Before any query plan is executed, the Sybase System XI optimizer has accomplished the following tasks:

- Estimated the number of 2K pages it needs to read for each table in the complete plan
- Determined the total cache(s) per table(s) and index(es)
- Determined the I/O size available to cache
- Determined the cache strategy needed by the target query
- Determined the access strategy: Scan vs. index type used (clustered or nonclustered)

CAUTION

The optimizer currently does not have an awareness of inter-related, con-current queries. This limitation arises because the optimizer is unaware of current total cache utilization.

3.3 SARG, a Key Optimizer Ingredient

The optimizer's ability to produce an efficient query plan depends upon the presence of a qualified search argument, which in Sybase parlance is known as a SARG (Search ARGument). The optimizer uses SARGs to determine whether or not to use a specific index. In fact, without a SARG located some-where in the body of a WHERE clause, the query plan will not use an index at all. See Figure 3.1.

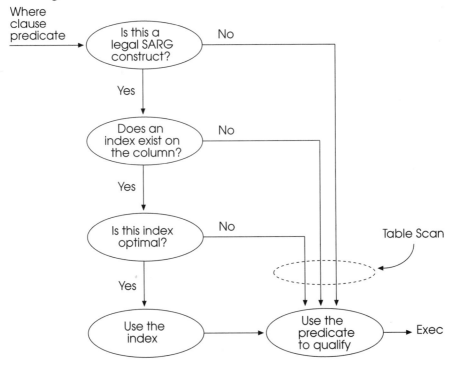

In this simple view of optimizer logic it can be clearly seen why the presence of a SARG is essential in theselection of an index.

Figure 3.1

Basic Optimizer Logical Flow

WARNING

The optimizer will not use an index without the presence of a search argument (SARG).

Sybase has specified the rules governing SARGs as follows:

- The clause must be of the form COLUMN OPERATOR EXPRESSION. The System XI optimizer also recognizes the reverse, EXPRESSION OPERATOR COLUMN as a SARG. The "is null" expression is treated like an OPERATOR EXPRESSION combination, and therefore is allowable as a SARG. See Figure 3.2.

COLUMN	OPERATOR	EXPRESSION
EXPRESSION	OPERATOR	COLUMN
COLUMN	IS NULL	

Figure 3.2
Legal SARG Structure

- The column referenced in the clause must be the first column in an index.
- There cannot be a calculation or function involved in the clause.

WARNING

Type conversion is implemented with a function. Therefore, implicit type conversions create a function call that destroys the SARG.

- The operator must belong to the following set: =, <, >, >=, <=, !>, !<, <>, !=, is null.   Note that the not equals operators can use a nonclustered index to scan the leaf index pages, but it cannot use the index to limit the search in the usual way. A nonclustered leaf index scan is always less costly than a data page scan because it only carries the index keys.

- The data types of both the expression and the column must match.

If the above criteria are not met, the clause is not a SARG in the eyes of Sybase and an index will not be used to satisfy the query. You can see that on a large table, a simple programming oversight can cause a major performance degradation when a missing SARG causes a table scan.

The optimizer will convert BETWEEN queries and some LIKE queries to range searches, but it will take time to do this. Therefore, it is best if you write them this way from the beginning.

See the performance tuning tactics chapter for hints regarding the use of SARGs for optimal performance.

3.4 OAM page: A Key Component for Optimizer Statistics

The optimizer goes directly to a table's Object Allocation Map (OAM) page to obtain information about data demographics. The purpose of the OAM page is to provide an optimum mechanism for allocating new space for database objects as they grow. See Figure 3.3. An individual OAM page may hold information on from 2,000 to 65,000 data or index objects. The optimizer is especially concerned with the number of rows in the table and the number of pages utilized. The optimizer requires these metrics in calculating optimum query strategies. These metrics are updated with each insert or delete of the target data or index object within the database system.

The optimizer uses index density metrics to evaluate the overall cost in joining tables. Because it is an automated tool, however, it can make mistakes and you, as a programmer, can use different tactics to change the optimizer's behavior. For example, it has been observed that over-qualification in the WHERE clause when both the join and the search argument involve the same column increases performance. It appears that this over-specification provides the optimizer with better density estimates. Here is an example of this behavior:

```
select a.department_code, department_name, subject_name
    from department a, subject b
    where a.department_code=b.department_code
    and a.department_code='cosc'
    and b.department_code='cosc'
```

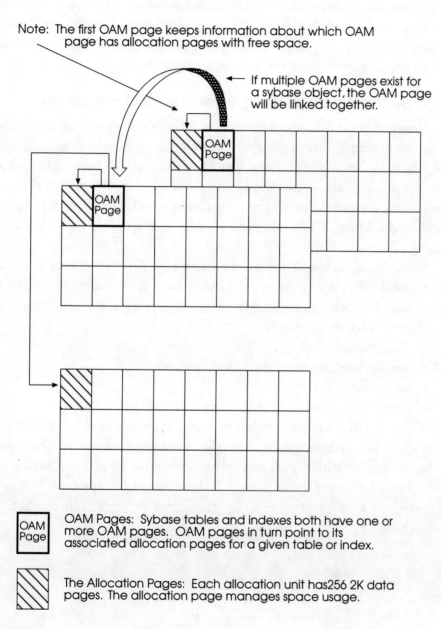

Note: The first OAM page keeps information about which OAM
       page has allocation pages with free space.

If multiple OAM pages exist for
a sybase object, the OAM page
will be linked together.

OAM Pages: Sybase tables and indexes both have one or
more OAM pages. OAM pages in turn point to its
associated allocation pages for a given table or index.

The Allocation Pages: Each allocation unit has 256 2K data
pages. The allocation page manages space usage.

Figure 3.3
How OAM and Allocation Pages Work Together to Assist Optimization

Notice that the second AND clause, **b.department_code='cosc'** is redundant, and should not be necessary. However, without it, the optimizer chooses an index on the department table but not on the subject table. For more information, see the performance tuning tactics chapter.

3.5 Understanding and Using Showplan for Optimization

Showplan is the Sybase mechanism for analyzing query plans generated by the Sybase System XI Server. You use Showplan to determine whether or not the optimizer is behaving rationally. Many new features have been added to improve the utility of Showplan. Showplan output was at one time very difficult to read, looking more like a pile of code than a report engineered for human consumption. Many of these deficiencies have been removed in the latest release.

Showplan dissects and exposes the query plan that the optimizer has selected for execution in a step-by-step manner. Each of these steps provides important clues as to why either the client or the server may be performing poorly.

Showplan has four sections:

- Basic showplan
- Specific components named by showplan
- Access method analysis
- Subquery analysis

The following examples of showplan sessions illustrate the basic ways in which showplan analyzes the decisions the optimizer has made. We have embedded comments within each example to give a line by line explanation of how to interpret the showplan output. The purpose of this approach is to give the reader a sense of what we feel is important for practical performance tuning strategies.

3.5.1   Showplan for a SELECT Statement

Listing 3.1 will help you in decoding Showplan output.

```
1> set Showplan on [see Note 1]
2> go
1> use college
2> go

1> select department_code,
2>     department_name,
3>     head_of_department
4> from department
5> where department_code="cosc"
6> go
```

[Showplan output follows]

```
QUERY PLAN FOR STATEMENT 1 (at line 2). [see Note 2]
STEP 1 [see Note 3]
The type of query is SELECT.
FROM TABLE [see Note 4]
department
Nested iteration.[see Note 5]
Using Clustered Index. [see Note 6]
Index: pk_department [see Note 7]
Ascending scan.
Positioning by key.
Keys are:
department_code
Using I/O Size 2 Kbytes.
```

Listing 3.1
Showplan for isql session SELECT (Page 1 of 2)

```
With LRU Buffer Replacement Strategy. [see Note 8]
department_code    department_name      head_of_department
---------------------------------------------------------
cosc               Computer Science   Dr. C.J. Date
(1 row affected)
```

Listing 3.1
Showplan for isql session SELECT (Page 2 of 2)

Note 1. This line begins showplan. "Set showplan off" is useful with a long script where you need to observe only one section.

Note 2. Statement 1 is first number of a batch set, "at line" is code line number within the batch stream.

Note 3. Every statement is numbered. Union statements start with new numbers on each side of the Union statement.

Note 4. FROM TABLE shows exactly which tables will be read. When an insert, delete, update or a select into is used, the table modified will show up as a TO TABLE (see below).

Note 5. The nomenclature of the technique used to join tables - of little importance.

Note 6. Pay attention to this. Often it is imperative to know whether you are using a clustered index.

Note 7. The name of the index is shown. It is very important to see which nonclustered index is being used. In this case, there is only one clustered index.

Note 8. This means that the pages read will be put on the beginning of the MRU/LRU chain, to be aged out normally, instead of "fetch and discard" (MRU). See the memory chapter for more information.

3.5.2   Showplan for a Two Table Join

The showplan for "join with a SARG" is shown in Listing 3.2.

```
select a.dept_code, a.dept_name,
    b.subject_name, b.credits
from dept a, subject b
where a.dept_code = b.dept_code
and a.dept_code = "biol"
QUERY PLAN FOR STATEMENT 1 (at line 2).
STEP 1
The type of query is SELECT.
FROM TABLE
department
Nested iteration.
Index : pk_dept [see Note 1]
Ascending scan.
Positioning by key.
Keys are:
dept_code
Using I/O Size 2 Kbytes.
With LRU Buffer Replacement Strategy.
FROM TABLE
subject
Nested iteration.
Table Scan. [see Note 2]
Ascending scan.
Positioning at start of table.
Using I/O Size 2 Kbytes.
With LRU Buffer Replacement Strategy.
dept_code    dept_name      subject_name      credits
```

Listing 3.2
Showplan for "Join with a SARG" (Page 1 of 2)

```
----------------------------------------------------------------
biol          Biology       Biology 101        4
biol          Biology       Biology 201        4
biol          Biology       Biology 301        5
biol          Biology       Biology 401        6
(4 rows affected)
```

Listing 3.2
Showplan for "Join with a SARG" (Page 2 of 2)

Note 1. Used a nonclustered index, nonclustered is implied, index name is
        specified. Notice the SARG after the "where...and" is of the form
        <column> <operator> <expression>. Without the SARG it would
        have SCANNED the table

Note 2. In this case there is neither an index nor a SARG to support it

3.5.3   Showplan for UPDATE

The showplan for UPDATE is shown in Listing 3.3.

```
update department
set head_of_department = "Prof. J.H. Johansen"
where department_code = "biol"
QUERY PLAN FOR STATEMENT 1 (at line 2).
STEP 1
The type of query is UPDATE.
The update mode is direct.
FROM TABLE
department
Nested iteration.
Index : pk_department [see Note 1]
Ascending scan. [see Note 2]
```

Listing 3.3
Showplan for UPDATE (Page 1 of 2)

```
Positioning by key.
Keys are:
department_code
Using I/O Size 2 Kbytes.
With LRU Buffer Replacement Strategy.
TO TABLE
department
(1 row affected)
```

Listing 3.3
Showplan for UPDATE (Page 2 of 2)

Note 1. This is good news. The index is being used.

Note 2. This line is of no practical importance. Do not be alarmed. All Sybase
scans are ascending, and this line simply reports the SCAN direction.
It does not mean a table is being scanned. If there is an Index indica-
tor everything is OK.

3.5.4   Showplan for INSERT INTO

The showplan for direct INSERT INTO is shown in Listing 3.4.

```
insert into department
(department_code, department_name, head_of_department)
values   ("geol", "Geology", "Prof. M. Suzmann")


QUERY PLAN FOR STATEMENT 1 (at line 2).


STEP 1
The type of query is INSERT.
The update mode is direct. [see Note 1]
TO TABLE
```

Listing 3.4
Showplan for direct INSERT INTO (Page 1 of 2)

```
department

. . .

(1 row affected)
```

Listing 3.4
Showplan for direct INSERT INTO (Page 2 of 2)

Note 1. The direct mode is preferred over the deferred mode. There are three
types of direct updates, the best is "update in place." Update in place
is much faster and, according to Sybase, generates fewer log writes.
Updates in place are desirable though they can be difficult to achieve
in a natural manner. As proof examine the list of demands for update
in place:

- The record length CANNOT change (no varchar, or nulls allowed)
- CANNOT be a member of a clustered index
- CANNOT be a participant of a key having referential integrity
- CANNOT have a join (in other words the update must be against
  a single table)
- There CANNOT be a trigger using the field for selection "...if up-
  date (last_name)..."
- The table cannot be used by the replication server

The first four Update In Place laws are difficult enough, but five and
six can be truly difficult to avoid.   However, the performance gains
are substantial. Using it will help when trying to build databases in a
symmetrical multi-processing environment. It facilitates the development of concurrent transactions against the database.

The problem is, the showplan does NOT tell whether an update in
place occurs. A direct update is either an update in place, using a
"cheap" replacement strategy or an "expensive" one, and there is no
way to tell from Showplan.

Sybase has improved update in place, separating delete/insert operations which are logged and maintaining the row in the same place if
at all possible. Row movement is prevented whenever possible, which
helps concurrency.

3.5.5   Showplan for SELECT INTO

The showplan for SELECT INTO is shown in Listing 3.5.

```
select * into temp_dept
from department
QUERY PLAN FOR STATEMENT 1 (at line 2).
STEP 1
The type of query is CREATE TABLE. [see Note 1]
STEP 2
The type of query is INSERT.
The update mode is direct. [see Note 2]
FROM TABLE
department
Nested iteration.
Table Scan. [see Note 3]
Ascending scan.
Positioning at start of table. [see Note 4]
Using I/O Size 2 Kbytes.
With LRU Buffer Replacement Strategy.
TO TABLE
temp_dept
(8 rows affected)
```

Listing 3.5
Showplan for SELECT INTO

Note 1. Note the creation of the temp_dept table

Note 2. Mode is direct because of the equality between the two tables, also note no indexes

Note 3. Since we are moving everything into temp_dept this is a good thing.

Note 4. This line announces the place where the scan begins. Some scans begin at the start of the first data hit.

3.5.6   Showplan for DROP TABLE

The showplan for DROP TABLE is shown in Listing 3.6.

```
drop table temp_dept
QUERY PLAN FOR STATEMENT 1 (at line 2).
STEP 1
The type of query is DROP TABLE. [see Note 1]
```

Listing 3.6
Showplan for DROP TABLE

Note 1. This is about as simple as it gets. The point is that Showplan reports
         that the statement is legitimate. If for some reason it could not run
         the statement it would tell you.

3.5.7   Showplan for DELETE

The showplan for DELETE is shown in Listing 3.7.

```
delete from department    [see Note 1]
where department_code = "geol" [see Note 2]
QUERY PLAN FOR STATEMENT 1 (at line 2).
STEP 1
The type of query is DELETE.
The update mode is deferred. [see Note 3]
FROM TABLE
department
Nested iteration.
```

Listing 3.7
Showplan for DELETE (Page 1 of 2)

```
Index : pk_department
Ascending scan.
Positioning by key.
Keys are:
department_code
Using I/O Size 2 Kbytes.
With LRU Buffer Replacement Strategy.
FROM TABLE
student
Table Scan. [see Note 4]
Ascending scan.
Positioning at start of table.
Using I/O Size 2 Kbytes.
With LRU Buffer Replacement Strategy.
FROM TABLE
subject
Table Scan. [see Note 4]
Ascending scan.
Positioning at start of table.
Using I/O Size 2 Kbytes.
With LRU Buffer Replacement Strategy.
FROM TABLE
teaching_staff
Table Scan. [see Note 4]
Ascending scan.
Positioning at start of table.
Using I/O Size 2 Kbytes.
With LRU Buffer Replacement Strategy.
TO TABLE
department
(1 row affected)
```

Listing 3.7
Showplan for DELETE (Page 2 of 2)

Note 1. This should serve as a clear example as to why you MUST run Showplans. Note that all we want to do is delete a record, but the Showplan is very complicated.

Note 2. This simple delete using a SARG will use the index but scan three tables. Look at the following code to see how this surprised us.

Note 3. With Deferred Mode the transaction log is read and written to twice. This is very slow.

Note 4. If constraints exist between tables with no index YOU WILL GET SCANS. When a foreign key constraint is created, Sybase does NOT automatically create an index. Other DBMSs do this; Sybase does not. You will need to specify indexes on foreign keys in a separate operation in order to improve performance here.

3.5.8   Showplan for ORDER BY

The showplan for ORDER BY is shown in Listing 3.8.

```
select * from department
order by department_code
QUERY PLAN FOR STATEMENT 1 (at line 2).
STEP 1
The type of query is INSERT.
The update mode is direct.
Worktable1 created for ORDER BY. [see Note 1]
FROM TABLE
department
Nested iteration.
Table Scan.
Ascending scan.
Positioning at start of table.
Using I/O Size 2 Kbytes.
With LRU Buffer Replacement Strategy.
TO TABLE
```

Listing 3.8
Showplan for ORDER BY (Page 1 of 2)

```
Worktable1.
STEP 2
The type of query is SELECT.
This step involves sorting. [see Note 2]
FROM TABLE
Worktable1.
Using GETSORTED
Table Scan. [see Note 3]
Ascending scan.
Positioning at start of table.
Using I/O Size 2 Kbytes.
With MRU Buffer Replacement Strategy.
 department_code    department_name      head_of_department
 -------------------------------------------------------------
  apma              Applied Math         Prof.R.Ronald
  bioc              Biochemistry         Dr.W.I.Smith
  biol              Biology              Prof.J.Johansen
  chem              Chemistry            Prof.A.Nobel
  cosc              Computer Science     Dr.C.J.Date
  math              Mathematics          Dr.G.Murphy
  phys              Physics              Prof.E.Johnson
 (7 rows affected)
```

Listing 3.8
Showplan for ORDER BY (Page 2 of 2)

Note 1. Creates a table in Tempdb. If this happens frequently in your applications and if performance is critical then it would be wise to look at moving the tempdb to a solid state device. Try to keep tempdb on a single contiguous device. Definitely assign tempdb to its own data cache. Use the following example of configuring the system with "sp_cacheconfig," "sp_bindcache," "temp_mem," "tempdb." Use ORDER BY judiciously, because creating tables in tempdb causes table locks. The locks can cause concurrency problems in the system tables if it goes on too often.

Note 2. Sorting too carries a heavy overhead price.

Note 3. The price being in the form of a table scan.

3.5.9   Showplan for GROUP BY

The showplan for GROUP BY is shown in Listing 3.9.

```
select calender_year, quarter, sum(payment_amt)
from payment
group by calender_year, quarter
QUERY PLAN FOR STATEMENT 1 (at line 2).
STEP 1
The type of query is SELECT (into Worktable1).
   [see Note 1]
GROUP BY
Evaluate Grouped SUM OR AVERAGE AGGREGATE.
FROM TABLE
payment
Nested iteration.
Table Scan.
Ascending scan.
Positioning at start of table.
Using I/O Size 2 Kbytes.
With LRU Buffer Replacement Strategy.
TO TABLE
Worktable1.
STEP 2
The type of query is SELECT.
FROM TABLE
Worktable1.
Nested iteration.
Table Scan. [see Note 2]
Ascending scan.
Positioning at start of table.
Using I/O Size 2 Kbytes.
```

Listing 3.9
Showplan for GROUP BY (Page 1 of 2)

```
With MRU Buffer Replacement Strategy.
calender_year                      quarter
---------------------------------------------------------
     1995 fall                     2,064.00
     1995 summer                   1,171.20
     1996 spring                   3,760.00
     1996 winter                   23,463.52
  (4 rows affected)
```

Listing 3.9
Showplan for GROUP BY (Page 2 of 2)

Note 1. Group by will create a worktable in tempdb with the same general problems as the ones associated with the order by.

Note 2. The work table is SCANNED.

3.6 Using DBCC TRACEON(3604, 302)

The TRACEON diagnostic tool is an essential weapon in the arsenal of a performance tuner. It provides inside information as to why the optimizer made specific choices. In addition, by examining DBCC output you can follow the performance analysis process of the optimizer in a stepwise fashion. This is the best way to understand the Sybase optimizer. DBCC is used as a diagnostic tool in the follow ways:

- As a debug tool: It can be used to debug queries in the passive sense.
- As a design tool: Proactively, it can be used to determine indexes, join orders, and search argument validity

> **WARNING**
> When using DBCC TRACEON(3604, 302) with stored procedures, you must execute with recompile.

The DBCC TRACEON command is executed from within isql. The following DBCC output in Listing 3.10 is annotated with our notes. The example file was submitted with DBCC TRACEON(3604, 302) embedded within the SQL batch file.

```
use college
dbcc traceon(3604, 302)
DBCC execution completed. If DBCC printed error messages,
contact a user with System Administrator (SA) role.
select * from student
where student_id_nbr = 7603140001


*******************************
Entering q_score_index() for table 'student'
    (objectid 537052949, varno = 0). [see Note 1]
The table has 21 rows and 1 pages. [see Note 2]
Scoring the SEARCH CLAUSE: [see Note 3]
student_id_nbr EQ [see Note 4]
Base cost: indid: 0 rows: 21 pages: 1 prefetch: N
    [see Note 5]
I/O size: 2 cacheid: 0 replace: LRU
Unique nonclustered index found—return rows 1 pages 3
Cheapest index is index 2, costing 3 pages and
generating 1 rows per scan, using no data prefetch
(size 2) on dcacheid 0 with LRU replacement
Search argument selectivity is 0.047619.
*******************************
student_id_nbr major  first_name
       middle_name     last_name
       date_of_birth  telephone_area_code telephone_nbr
-------------- ----- -----------------------------
       ------------------------------- --------------------
       ----------------------- ---------------- ------------
7603140001     chem  Tony
```

Listing 3.10
Example of DBCC output (Page 1 of 2)

```
    NULL                          Goodsell
      Mar 14 1976 12:00AM      515               5553378
    (1 row affected)
    dbcc traceoff(3604, 302)
    DBCC execution completed. If DBCC printed error messages,
    contact a user with System Administrator (SA) role.
```

Listing 3.10
Example of DBCC output (Page 2 of 2)

Note 1. The q_score_index() routine determines the cost of the index choice for tables in which it found a SARG. Varno is the order that the optimizer uses for the tables it finds in the FROM clause. This order may be different from the order in your from clause. If you are developing for a heterogeneous environment, you may consider reorganizing your FROM clause tables. This may help when encountering weaker optimizers of other RDBMSs.

Note 2. Row counts should be scrutinized, as they may be wrong. Row counts are derived from the System tables. If there is a real inconsistency problem, the optimizer may be making incorrect query plans.

Note 3. LOOK FOR THE ABSENCE OF THIS SECTION. The absence of this section means that you have developed a query without a valid SARG or a join clause. There is one exception: When a non-clustered index provides coverage. If a search argument does not appear within this section, the optimizer is not using it. Therefore re-analyze the need for its presence within the WHERE clause. Any join clause that does not appear within this section is in jeopardy and should be cause for alarm.

Note 4. EQ is the evaluation code of the search clause. See below for the domain listing for evaluation codes.

Note 5. Use the Base cost section to validate accurate row counts and page counts. They can be validated by the use of SET STATISTICS IO ON and SELECT * from table. We recommend developing a DBA utility to perform this calculation when required.

Evaluation code	Evaluation long name
EQ	Equality (=)
LT	Less than (<)
LE	Less than or equal to (<=)
GT	Greater than (>)
GE	Greater than or equal to (>=)
NE	Not equals (!=)
ISNULL	Is null evaluation
ISNOTNULL	Is not null evaluation

Table 3.1
Evaluation Domain Table

3.7 Techniques to Use When You Know Better

Sybase has always had "undocumented features" which enable you to force the optimizer to do something that it would not ordinarily choose to do. In System XI, Sybase has provided several new techniques to help outsmart the optimizer. As you might imagine, a certain amount of care is required when using these techniques. You should verify that you really are smarter than it. Run showplan and statistics time to make sure the results really are faster. See the performance tuning tactics chapter for details on how to use these diagnostic tools.

3.7.1   Understanding and Using Forceplan for Optimization

The Forceplan command, as the name implies, forces a join of tables in the order given in the FROM clause. Sybase warns their users strongly against the use of Forceplan, and so do we. However we also acknowledge that sometimes there is no other alternative. In these cases we extend an additional admonishment. Bring all Forceplan code under strict configuration management techniques. This will help you when the problematic data structures or data instances shift. The only constant in the database world is change. Therefore, be prepared, especially with this type of code.

The following listing demonstrates the use of Forceplan:

```
Use college
go
Set forceplan on
go
select *
from Table_myway  C, Table_areusure  A, Table_lastchnc B
where ...
Set forceplan off
```

Using an example similar to this, execute DBCC TRACEON(3604, 302) and showplan with Forceplan and without Forceplan, to observe the optimizer at work.

CAUTION

Do not forget to turn forceplan off after the specific query. If you don't, it will be in effect for the rest of the session, and all subsequent queries will be in jeopardy of slow performance due to inappropriate indexes being used.

HINT

Do not forget to run update statistics. Sometimes the optimizer is not doing what you expect simply because the statistics haven't been updated recently. Run update statistics at a low activity time in your workplace cycle, however, as it takes a table level lock.

3.7.2   Forcing Index Usage

If there is a specific index that you want the optimizer to use, you can indicate it in parentheses after the table list in the FROM clause:

```
use college
go
select last_name, first_name, class_id, grade
```

```
from student, grade (index stud_name)
where student.student_id = grade.student_id
and last_name="Smith"
and first_name="Mary"
go
```

To use this technique you must know your data demographics. The usefulness of an index may change over time, as the distribution of the data varies with respect to the key. Forcing the optimizer to use an index today may not be as effective six months from now.

3.7.3   Avoiding the Four Table Rule

Sybase has always used the "four table rule" when the optimizer considers query plans. It always looks at combinations of four tables at a time. There are times when the optimizer will overlook a useful query plan because of this rule.

Earlier releases of SQL Server could be "helped" by listing the tables in the FROM clause in the order of selectivity (most selective on the search argument first). In System XI, this is not the case. System XI considers many different combinations of four tables, but four continues to be the magic number.

If you suspect that the best query plan might be overlooked because of the four table rule, you can override it and tell the optimizer to consider a larger number of tables together. Use "set table count":

```
set table count 5
go
select s.last_name, s.first_name,
   department_name, subject_name,
   quarter, calendar_year,  instructor=t.last_name
   from student s, grade g, class c, subject sb,
   department d, teaching_staff t
   where  s.student_id=g.student_id
   and g.class_id=c.class_id
   and c.subject_code=sb.subject_code
   and sb.department_code=d.department_code
   and c.staff_id_nbr=staff_id_nbr
   and d.department_code="cosc"
   and calendar_year="1995"
```

```
go

set table count 4

go
```

Look at what the optimizer is doing by using DBCC TRACEON (302), Showplan and statistics. Don't forget to use diagnostics before and after applying forcing techniques.

3.8 Clauses

There are four distinct types of clauses in SQL:

- Search Argument Clause
- Join Clause
- OR Clause
- Subquery Clause

These four clauses form the heart of SQL and have a tremendous effect on the performance of a production system. The optimizer focuses its attention on the contents of these clauses to develop query plans. When tuning queries, most of your performance strategies and tactics will use the elements of one or more of these clauses.

3.8.1   Search Argument Clause

In Sybase literature, the clause containing the search argument is often labeled the search clause. The search clause provides selectivity within the WHERE clause. It is the single most important factor in the optimizer's selection of an index. Sybase documentation states that without the search argument (SARG) the optimizer will select no index.

In pre-System XI releases, search arguments had to be written with the column id on the left hand side of the SARG to be effective. That restriction is no longer true in System XI. A SARG must be in one of the following forms:

<column> <operator> <expression>

<expression> <operator> <column>

<column> is null

The following facts will help you to enhance the optimization of a search clause:

- Make sure that your code contains a valid SARG.

- The selection process is based on statistics kept on the OAM Page. Run update statistics often in accordance with the frequency of inserts and updates.
- Remember that the selectivity of the first column is most important.
- Use Showplan to indicate index usage. Showplan will reveal whether or not your SARG is causing the proper index to be chosen.
- Run DBCC TRACEON (3406, 302) if you think the SARG should be causing an index to be chosen and it is not being utilized.

A typical example of DBCC TRACEON (3406, 302) is shown in Listing 3.10.

CAUTION

Mismatched datatypes can cause sever performance problems because they destroy SARGs. It is easy to overlook them during development.

3.8.2   Join Clause

The purpose of the join clause is to join one or more tables together using similar attributes.   No other SQL statement better exemplifies the relational concept than the Join clause. The key to performance lies in your ability to write optimizable Join Clauses. Keep the following points in mind.

- Overspecify all Join relationships. The Sybase optimizer does not yet support the closely related concepts of transitive closure or associative closure; by overspecifying you give the optimizer a better chance of understanding relationships.

Transitive Closure example:

```
If class.tuition = course.cost and
   class.tuition < $1000 then
   it follows that course.cost is < $1000.
```

While this statement is true and makes sense to most people, the optimizer does not yet understand this logic.

Associative Closure example:

```
If class.tuition = 100 and
   course.cost = class.tuition
   then it follows that course.cost = 100.
```

Here too the optimizer is unable to understand the logical connection. The following example demonstrates overspecification:

```
SELECT * FROM personnel p, teaching_staff TS
    WHERE p.ssn = TS.staff_id_nbr and
        p.first_name = TS.first_name and
        TS.first_name like 'FRE%'
```

- Pay attention to join order because it is important to the optimizer. Use Showplan to prove that the join clause is working as you expect.
- Keep in mind that the optimizer uses density estimation from the OAM page analysis to produce the optimized query plan. Therefore, the more columns in the join, the better the estimate.

3.8.3   OR Clause

The OR clause is perhaps the most problematic of all SQL statements because it is difficult to optimize. Observing the following unpredictable optimizer behavior:

- The optimizer has a tendency to convert an IN operator to an OR. This means that you must be careful to perform Showplan analysis on all IN operator driven statements.
- Because the OR clause can create dynamic indexes, SCANS may be unavoidable.

For examples and suggestions, see the performance tuning tactics chapter.

WARNING
Using the OR clause may cause unavoidable table scans.

3.8.4   Subquery Clause

A Subquery is a query nested within the WHERE or HAVING clause of another query. A subquery provides the results of the inner query to the outer query and is used when the outer most query needs the results of another query to perform its work. In System XI, subquery optimization has improved dramatically. However, avoid Subquery processing in System 10 at all costs. It is very slow. If you are using version 4.9.x and your applications include numerous subqueries, upgrade directly to System XI.

The new extended optimization strategies for subqueries revolve around the following notions:

1. Creating a Tempdb worktable to store subquery results
2. Converting subqueries into joins
3. Improved execution order
4. Improved usage of cache

The first strategy (named *materialization* by Sybase), executes the subquery and creates a worktable in which the results are placed. The server then takes the outer query and joins the results to the worktable. The optimizer improves performance by employing this strategy.

Converting subqueries into joins "flattens" the quantifiable predicate subqueries "in," "any," and "exists." When the optimizer encounters a subquery using any of the aforementioned predicates, it builds a set of equijoins. As soon as the query tests true, the search terminates.

There are occasions where a WHERE clause is required within the body of the subquery. When this happens, it is not always necessary to execute the inner query. The optimizer now realizes this, and decides when to execute the subquery.

Finally, when the optimizer cannot improve the subquery by any of the new methods, it attempts to use in-memory cache. According to Sybase, this technique does not help when there are no correlated values between the subquery components.

For more information about the new subquery processing techniques, see the Sybase SQL Server Performance and Tuning Guide (part of System XI documentation).

EXECUTION THREAD ANALYSIS

4

This chapter presents a practical strategy that uses execution thread analysis to provide the basis for concurrent systems performance tuning. An *execution thread* is a sequential chain of called procedures or transactions that require end-to-end completion.

The methodology enables you to find the transactions that will yield the most benefit from optimization, and therefore warrant intensive tuning. It sets a framework for analysis, and lets you get the best "bang for the buck" from your efforts. It prevents "analysis paralysis," and allows you to spend your time and effort only on those transactions that will yield the greatest return.

This set of proven methods and techniques works without regard to any specific optimizer or DBMS. It is especially applicable to client/server environments, where concurrency is a key issue. However, the solution to a Sybase tuning problem is governed by the specific technical nuances of the Sybase kernel and optimizer.

The authors believe that the benefits gained by employing these techniques go beyond performance gains themselves (although these gains can be substantial). This approach enhances overall software quality by promoting scalability. When the number of users and transactions grows, a well-designed database will be resilient enough to handle the growth gracefully.

4.1 Concurrency Anomalies

Contention is one of the most important problems found in a large multi-user client/server environment. Contention occurs when a transaction needs to use a page on which another transaction has a lock, and almost always results from poor design. Locks are very important to data integrity because they prevent data corruption. However, every time a lock is taken it has the potential to cause poor performance for other users who have to wait for the locks to be released.

Long transactions involving locks are especially problematic in the Sybase environment. The problem is exacerbated by Sybase's use of page locking rather than row locking—a long transaction can lock many pages and hold them for an extended period of time. In the process, other users needing to use those pages must wait. In a system with hundreds or thousands of users, it is easy to see that a set of locks on a critical portion of the database can block potentially hundreds of users. Even something as simple as the transaction log can cause unexpected problems in this sort of environment. Long running transactions prevent the dump of completed transactions and therefore the log can overflow.

Transactions which access highly volatile, highly used tables should be your first target for analysis. There are many strategies to aid in transaction tuning, but first you must decide which transactions to examine to yield maximum improvement. The following section will help you to learn where to look.

WARNING
Always benchmark before and after you optimize so you can prove performance gains. Never take a users' word at face value when it comes to performance issues, because perception may be different from reality. Management normally demands proof of performance gains, and with accurate benchmarks you can gain their support. With an accurate benchmark in hand, you can easily justify the time and effort required to tune a transaction.

4.2 Execution Thread Analysis

Imagine that you are faced with a database that has a clear performance problem. Your benchmarks show that performance in a critical area of the system is falling, and users are beginning to grumble. If you have the resources available, the two-team approach lets you attack the problem on different fronts simultaneously. Even if you do not have the resources, you can use the approach but take on the different roles of the two teams as you work through the problem.

In the two-team approach, the first team is the "Fast Route Team." It will realize excellent performance gains immediately. The second team, known as the "Execution Thread Team," goes about a more thorough analysis to find more elusive problems and to assure quality throughout the modified environment.

Teams should be comprised of a mix of developers who know the specific applications involved, T-SQL coding experts who know and understand the nuances of the Sybase optimizer and who can write efficient SQL code, and database experts in the organization who understand physical database design, index optimization and server tuning issues.

The Fast Route team should perform the following tasks:

1. Create and run a simple script which lists all tables, the number of indexes on those tables, and number of rows.

2. List the tables with the following attributes:

   • The largest volume and the largest number of indexes

   • The largest volume and lowest number indexes

   • All tables with no index and 500 or more rows

Dense tables with numerous indexes are what we affectionately refer to as the "Fat Cows," and these tables are the best place to start looking for problems. Large tables with a low number of indexes may benefit from indexing and are therefore a good place to look for problems as well.

3. Analyze the indexes of all the fat cow tables. Some indexes may be duplicates of others and can therefore be eliminated, while other indexes can be combined. Analyze the key for the clustered index, and consult with the developers on the team who know the application to determine whether this key is justified. Check for indexes on common search fields and foreign keys and eliminate them where possible. The overall goal is to reduce the number of indices supported and maintained on a specific table to a minimum. Benchmark the application before and after this

first pass. You will probably see a substantial performance gain right away if the database has not been tuned recently.

4. Gather in all source code for the domain chosen for optimization (functional area, application, etc.).

5. Scan the source code for all accesses to the fat cow tables. There are tools that assist you in scanning code, or you can write a simple utility to do this. Isolate these modules, stored procedures, etc. Separate the T-SQL code in the module from other code if the T-SQL is embedded in a host language or 4GL.

6. Have a T-SQL expert from the team analyze the T-SQL for clumsy code. Look for general inefficiencies like unnecessary temp table usage, use of NOT, OR, etc., and the absence of SARGs. In addition, look for implicit data type conversions in the various clauses of the SQL statement. These conversions can be extremely expensive, especially on large tables. Tune what you find and benchmark.

At this point, some real performance gains should have been realized. You will probably find and fix about 60% of the problems with this "fast" approach. This may be enough, and the users may be satisfied with the improvements made. However, if better performance is needed, you should continue with the Execution Thread Team approach. This approach is very thorough and will take time. Make sure that everyone knows beforehand that this is a methodical and disciplined approach, and there is an associated cost. You must decide if the cost is worth the benefit; we firmly believe that it is.

The Execution Thread Team should perform the following tasks:

1. Use a Business Model if one exists and determine the main functional groupings in the application. Determine the functional groups with high data usage, high volume, high cost and high visibility.

2. Choose the best functional area to work on, based on the factors mentioned in #1. Gather all code associated with this functional group; nothing must escape. Pay attention to modules "behind the scenes," C code, trigger code, etc.

3. Create an execution thread map, which diagrams each module/transaction and shows the links between them. In this map you will note relationships: Main code module A calls stored procedure B which fires

trigger C, etc. There are tools on the market which assist in doing this, one such being the ViewServer Database Process Flow Analyzer. This process is extremely time consuming, but will pay off later. Everyone should expect this phase to involve quite a bit of work.

VERY IMPORTANT
Do not forget about "side effects." For example, a database may contain triggers which are called from a data change event in another module. It may not seem at first glance that these two modules interact in any way. Your goal is to find this sort of hidden interaction. This hidden code is the most common problem when doing concurrency analysis—you forget about code that is not readily apparent, and it is this very code which turns out to be the Fat Cow bogging down the system. Realize that many threads may encompass code outside of the current target subject area. You still must include this code in your analysis. See Figure 4.1.

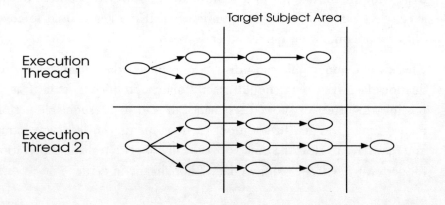

Figure 4.1
Transactions may lie outside of the scope of the target subject area. Do not ignore these transactions in your analysis.

4. Look at the most important threads in the application: those involving Fat Cow tables. Analyze Fat Cow usage throughout the thread. Build a "where used/how used" matrix to help with this process. Examine each

access to any Fat Cow table. Use Showplan, traceflag 302 and analyze whether indexes are used effectively. Create a spreadsheet which illustrates index usage for each query. Employ the micro tuning techniques outlined in the tuning chapter to carefully optimize the Fat Cow table accesses.

5.   Consider physical design strategies for each Fat Cow table. Can you slice a large table into smaller tables? Can you horizontally partition a table based on time and data aging? For instance, can you segregate sales data into separate tables by month, quarter or year? Sometimes the only way to handle Fat Cows is to slice them into pieces.

6.   Check index keys for selectivity in all Fat Cow composite indexes by testing the index by hand. After adding each key to the index, you should see significantly less volume and a large increase in selectivity. For instance, the first key in the index might retrieve 15,000 rows. After adding the next key you might see 100 rows. Qualify it further with the third key and you might see 60 rows. Because there is no significant gain in selectivity with the third key, you can eliminate it. However, you need to balance selectivity with covering requirements. If the key is used to cover one or more important queries, then leave it.

7.   Check the demographics and distribution of test data against real production data. Test data should exactly match production data if at all possible. Incorrect or skewed test data can lead to irresponsible performance tuning results. In addition, cache contents can lead you astray. You may have to clear the cache occasionally to get a realistic expectation for performance if the required data is not already in cache.

HINT

If you are using named caches in System XI, you can clear the cache by unbinding it, then binding it again. If you are using the default cache, you may have to reboot the server. Filling cache by using a very large select may work, but you cannot guarantee that ALL the data in cache was pushed out.

8. Employ a specialized team of programmers, referred to as "transaction choppers." This team is made up of business people, database wizards and SQL gurus. The goal of the team is to analyze the longest thread looking for creative ways to break it down into smaller logical units of work. This technique must reference the business rules to verify that they will remain in force. We recommend that the business rules be cross referenced according to transaction so that you have a list of the rules while you work on the logic involved in the transaction. The business people on the team are essential because they offer insight into the business rules and can verify the result of the transaction chopping process. Additionally look at eliminating unnecessary steps that may occur when multiple programmers develop a series of stored procedures.

9. Examine several threads simultaneously from a "common access strategy" point of view. Can the threads share the same indexes? Can you combine two indexes into one, and allow several transactions use the same index? Do the types of accesses merit large I/O? Fat Cows should have their own named cache so that they do not compete with other tables for memory. If they do not you should consider creating such a cache. If each select statement fetches a large number of rows (e.g., range searches or covered queries where consecutive data pages are fetched at once) then configure the named cache with a larger I/O pool size. See the memory chapter for more details.

10. Next, perform workflow analysis. This step requires a business person who is knowledgeable in the business and skilled in workflow analysis. Decide which transactions should occur when and optimize.

11. Use Transaction Maps to get a sense for time of day concurrency analysis and volumetrics. This step will assist the workflow analysis by providing a diagrammatic representation of the different tasks performed and their relative timing.

4.3 Transaction Maps and Concurrency

Modify the transaction process flow diagram that you created earlier to include the execution frequency of each transaction. You will want to include the maximum frequency at which each transaction occurs, as shown in Figure 4.2.

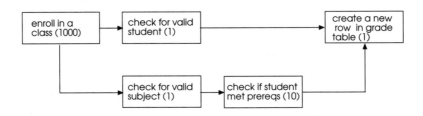

Figure 4.2

The transaction map above shows that the maximum number of times that the "En-roll in a class" thread is executed is 1000 times. It calls the smaller transactions at the rates shown.

Analyze your database looking for time of day or cyclical hot spots. Sales applications have typical "end of the month" or "end of the quarter" activity while a weekly time sheet application sees most of its activity on Monday morning or Friday afternoon. Determine what can be done to help these hot spots by asking questions like the following:

- Can you make more CPU resources available for them for these times of the day? Analyze how the application is written with respect to the data elements involved.

- Can you use lookup tables?

- Can you replace monotonically increasing primary keys with an alternative non-monotonically increasing key?

- Can you modify the locking pattern? Are there locks being held for a long time which prevent other inserts?

- Can you release the lock sooner on your increment table?

You can encapsulate the called transactions and show time of day and concurrency. Time of day can also be based upon time of month, quarter, semester, etc. For instance, the high rate of concurrency for enrolling students in classes is at the end and beginning of quarters. When this happens, most students enroll in classes either first thing in the morning or late in the afternoon:

Time of Day	Volume
8-9am	200
9-10am	1000
10-11am	500
11-12pm	100
12-1pm	200
1-2pm	200
2-3pm	300
3-4	600

Table 4.1
Transaction volume by time of day

Other volumetrics that are interesting to look at are estimates of how many times the transaction is executed based upon other table data. For instance, each student takes about 4 classes per quarter, but may have to execute the enrollment transaction several times per class (enroll in one, change the schedule and de-enroll in that class, then enroll in a different class, etc.)

Metrics like these can be captured by auditing tools, or you can create your own code to do it. You can use Sybase-supplied auditing tools, or you can use triggers or an open server to intercept execution and record it in a log.

Analyze all other concurrent transactions per time of day. Determine what other processing is happening at the end of or beginning of a quarter. Create a transaction map, like the one shown in Figure 4.3, which shows the high level transactions and their frequency of executed per time of day. Include high estimates for the maximum number of processes executing each transaction.

Once you determine the peak time of day (week, month, year) for your system, look for processes not dependent upon the time of day and shift them to times with less concurrent activity. For example, you might buffer low-priority transactions in a queue and process them from the queue at night to shift them away from a critical time that occurs every afternoon. Analyze whether your major execution threads can be staggered so they do not all execute at the same time, aligning these changes with the business and its needs. A workflow engineer's input will be valuable in making sure that your business rules and your database design mesh.

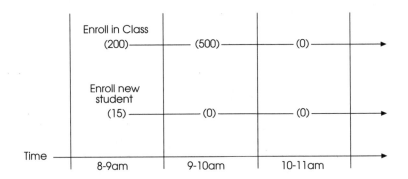

Figure 4.3
This kind of transaction map will help you get a handle on concurrent processes. 200 class enrollments along with15 new student enrollments occurred between 8-9am. Between 9-10am 500 more class enrollments were made, while between 10-11am enrollments came to a stand still.

You can also use your transaction map to look for possible conflicts between the concurrent transactions, such as deadlock contention.

4.4 Business Rules

One of the most important tasks in systems design involves analyzing and discovering the business rules. Business rules govern the business and lie at the heart of any enterprise model represented in a database application. Once you capture the business rules, they become essential to every aspect of system implementation.

Business rules are extremely valuable for execution thread analysis. They facilitate the examination and interrogation of each thread's value to the business. They help to prioritize the thread's position in the business. They can tell you how important a particular thread is to the overall goals and concerns of the enterprise. There is no need to waste time and energy performing a task and storing data if it has little value to add to the central mission of the business. You do not want to deliver a system which does nothing of interest.

You can therefore use business rules to trim the system of superfluous tasks. Sometimes entire transactions or large portions of the database can be eliminated because they do not support the business in a useful way. This fact of life explains why business process re-engineering—BPR—can be such an important aid to system design. Do not design a system that supports sub-optimal processes.

Business rules play a central role in transaction analysis, workflow analysis, and transaction chopping. Understand the rules enforced by the transactions, and make sure that any re-design that you do in the name of performance enhancement supports the rules. The business rules check the validity of the re-design, and ensure its quality. Performance must never compromise rule integrity.

4.5 Summary

It is important to view sophisticated database applications as systems of many variables interacting with one another. Concurrency is a widespread problem in such a system and requires careful analysis. Many factors affect concurrency, and this is why entire execution threads need to be analyzed in different ways. It is essential to consider concurrency and transaction design in performance tuning.

‖NDEXES

5

The indexing scheme used in a database has the biggest effect on search performance. The purpose of an index is to eliminate sequential searching (table scans) and provide an optimal search path to retrieve requested data. In the context of a DBMS, indexes have two goals:

- To provide for identification and uniqueness.
- To optimize access and retrieval time.

The programmer structures queries to perform searches in one of three ways:

- Primary key
- Foreign key
- Non-key search columns

You should build indexes with these three different kinds of searches in mind. An index tailored for the third type of search is sometimes called an "inverted entry index" because it positions the search in the middle of the data (inside-out).

Indexes are important to primary and foreign keys, where they are critical in facilitating and upholding referential integrity. For example, if you have a database design which contains a base table and multiple characteristic tables, a simple delete cascade could be very time consuming without the presence of indexes.

The design of an index strategy should draw heavily from three main sources:

- the conceptual data model, highlighting business rules
- the logical data model, highlighting referential integrity
- application requirements, highlighting performance

5.1 Index and Concurrency Issues

The following sections discuss Sybase index types. We will outline the goals of each in cost/benefit style and then relate the concurrency issues.

5.1.1   Clustered Indexes

A clustered index stores the data in the order dictated by the index. Sybase utilizes a true sparse index, in that the leaf node of the index is the actual data page. This design enables the server to eliminate one level of I/O.

The clustered index has special significance to the database design. The clustered index is especially good for queries that need to read large contiguous sections of the target table. Since all of the contiguous rows in the index physically exist next to one another on the drive, it is much more efficient to read through them sequentially. In a nonclustered index, any new row is added at the end of the table, so the rows exist on disk in a random order.

It is common for a clustered index to handle primary key responsibilities. Recall that primary keys must uniquely identify the record. This is often accomplished with some type of monotonically increasing value. This approach causes contention on the last page, just like a heap table with no indexes, and can lead to poor insertion performance. The identity column will give you fast system-generated unique identifier. This will help, but not completely alleviate the problem.

You should avoid the use of clustered indexes on a key value containing duplicates, as they can cause severe performance problems. Duplicate values will produce multiple overflow pages, which effectively reduces the efficiency of the index.

5.1.2   Heap Table with No Clustered Index

A table with no clustered index is called a heap. In a heap the database inserts all new rows on the last page of the table. This causes a classic concurrency problem when many processes need to insert. All of the processes end up block-ing each other as they try to simultaneously lock the last page. This problem can become a benefit in System XI. You can partition an insert-intensive table into physical segments. This approach allows the server to use several "last pag-es." Sybase randomly distributes each inserted row to a different page and ef-fectively eliminates the concurrency problem described above. When you use this technique you give up the opportunity to have a clustered index; you can-not use table partitions and a clustered index on the same table in System XI.

5.1.3   Nonclustered Index

A nonclustered index maintains pointers to the data pages containing the rows. The index structure contains only the key values. A nonclustered index is good for queries where you desire small, distinct portion of table (20% or less) is desired. Since a table can have only one clustered index, every other index on a table must be nonclustered.

Nonclustered indexes take up space and hurt insertion performance. On the other hand, they can significantly improve query performance. You goal in index design, therefore is to balance insertion performance, query perfor-mance, and database size. Factors to keep in mind when designing indexes:

- Statistics are kept on only the first field of any index. It is therefore very important that you make the first field as selective (as close to unique) as possible. The first field should also be the most useful: the field ac-cessed the most, searched on the most, etc.

- The combination of all keys which make up the index should be as se-lective (as close to unique) as possible. Each field should contribute sig-nificantly to "narrowing down" the values in a search. If a field does not add in this way, consider taking it out unless it covers important que-ries.

There is no limit to the number of nonclustered indexes. However, Sybase recommends that for symmetrical multi-processing environments you have no more than three nonclustered indexes per table. Although a large number of in-dexes can sometimes improve performance in decision support systems, there is a drawback. Indexes dramatically increase insertion/deletion overhead be-cause Sybase must update every index.

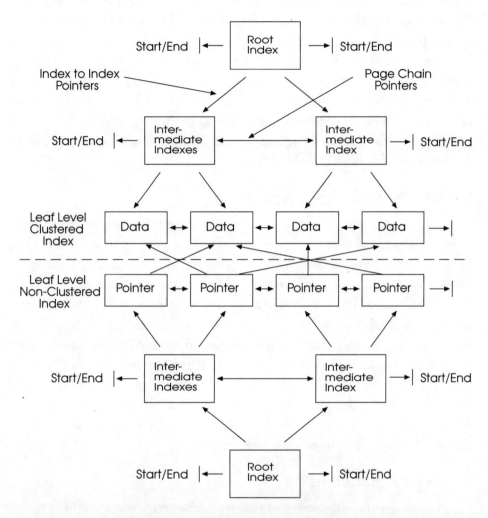

Note: The major difference between clustered and non-clustered indexes is that the clustered index ends with data at the leaf level while the non-clustered index ends with a pointer to the data.

Figure 5.1
Clustered and Non-Clustered Indexes

5.2 Using Nonclustered Indexes for Coverage

When you create a nonclustered index that contains several attributes designed to cover all the data requirements of a query, you are *covering* the query.

If a query uses this index and finds all of the data contained in the index, then the query never needs to access the data table. Not only do you save one level of I/O, but this nonclustered index can behave like a clustered index. Data is returned in the order required without having to do an "order by," and you eliminate the need for a costly worktable. Even a complete index scan (if needed) is not as costly as a table scan because the index records are not as long. They do not carry all of the other data values found in the table itself.

The benefits derived from covering can be substantial, and you should use the technique whenever possible.

5.3 Why Different Index Types?

Often in the design process, the decision to use a clustered or nonclustered index is not a trivial one. There are different data access strategies, and the two different index types satisfy different requirements. The delicate balance between retrieval and update performance is central to index design.

The clustered index offers faster retrieval of table data. An obvious problem associated with clustered indexes involves the movement of physical data. If the environment requires frequent inserts, updates and deletes then clustered indexes may impact write performance, especially when page splitting becomes excessive. However, the retrieval benefit usually outweighs the update penalty. You must carefully choose the key for the clustered index. In general, most tables should have a clustered index, and the key chosen for the index should be the one that gives maximum query performance.

5.4 Index Characteristics

Because of the importance of indexes in the performance tuning process, it is useful to keep the following characteristics in mind when designing indexes.

- Indexes are physical objects that occupy physical space in the database. Indexes take up as much space as its member attributes demand, combined with the space needed for page chain pointer. It is extremely easy to forget about the space requirements of indexes. For example, one client had a large database consisting of roughly 350 tables which represented a single instance of what was planned to be a globally distributed database system. The 350 table database had over 1000 indexes. The

DBAs complained vehemently, and inserts and updates brought the system to its knees. Concurrency anomalies were common. Although indexes are important to the performance of the database, you must use them judiciously. Careful analysis, as described in the chapter on execution thread analysis, is essential.

- Page splitting is a major concern for clustered indexes, but it affects the index structure of both kinds of indexes. If during insertion a row requires an index entry on a page that is full, a page split occurs. The database aligns page pointers to accommodate the new page, and this effort has a detrimental effect on performance. Page splitting is also a concurrency problem, because all the pages affected receive an exclusive lock. It slows down the write operation while all indexes and pages update. If a table is subject to many inserts, you can use fillfactor to avoid page splitting. Fillfactor leaves a portion of the page free, allowing the insertion of new rows without having to split the page. You can use fillfactor for both clustered indexes (including the data page) and nonclustered indexes, but it will not effect the data page for nonclustered index. For more information on fillfactor, see the chapter on locking.

- The goal of an index is to provide faster retrieval time. If the optimizer chooses the index, it will enable the query to execute faster. See the optimizer chapter for more information about how the optimizer makes decisions about which indexes to use, and how you can help persuade it to make the decisions you want.

- Indexes Enforce Uniqueness. There is no other way in Sybase to enforce uniqueness except through an index. The UNIQUE constraint creates an index "behind the scenes" to do this. You should pay particular attention to the Identity column. The column which uses the Identity must also be declared unique for it to be guaranteed. It is possible to "set identity insert on" and insert two non-unique values into the field, and the server will allow it if no unique index is used.

- Index selectivity is very important to the optimizer. The optimizer selects the index based on the selectivity of the leading column of the index. Therefore, make sure your selection of the first field agrees with the search argument (SARG) in the WHERE clause for the most important queries. Test with Showplan and the DBCC 302 trace flag. See the optimizer chapter for details.

- Design Indexes Carefully. Indexes are as much an object of design as any table. You must know the business rules in order to design indexes effectively.

5.5 Index Statistics are Important

Sybase maintains information about data demographics to help the optimizer make its decisions. In order for the optimizer to make correct decisions about the use of indexes, it must have good statistical data. You must therefore update statistics when you update the data. Not doing so can kill performance. The larger the table, the more important statistics become. Correct statistics heighten the optimizer's chances of choosing the most appropriate index to handle a query.

Unfortunately, Update Statistics performs a table scan to gather statistics for use by the optimizer, and holds exclusive table locks while it is scanning. Update statistics during lulls in activity to avoid performance degradation.

Use the DBCC TRACEON(3604, 302) tool to see what's going on between the optimizer and the available indexes. See the optimizer chapter for more information.

5.6 Index Tuning Strategy

If you have a system that is having significant performance problems, a good first step is to analyze the use of indexes. The index tuning strategy outlined here is aggressive and gives the tuner a good idea of where to find system hot spots. You can use this strategy in conjunction with execution thread analysis or alone for index analysis.

In order to use this strategy you need to create a sandbox. See Chapter 1 for details. Take the following steps:

1. Get counts on the total numbers of tables and indexes within the databases.

2. Locate all application system and subsystem source code. Ensure that there are no other access points to the database. Note that if your system allows ad-hoc queries, your only recourse may be user awareness training.

3. Isolate SQL and lib calls.

4. List all database tables and indexes. Use this listing to gain an understanding of table volume and related index size. This listing will give you an initial feeling for potential bottlenecks. This listing should show the following:
   - table name
   - number of indexes
   - table record count

5. List the tables with following attributes:
   - the largest volume and the largest number of indexes.
   - the largest volume and lowest indexes
   - all tables with no index and 500 or more rows

6. Parse source code to list any and all SQL access.

7. Check the target TEST database for production equivalent metrics.

8. Isolate SQL access code from the parsed listing and develop modules suitable for testing.

9. Methodically execute test modules using:
   - Set noexec on
   - Set Showplan on
   - DBCC TRACEON (3604, 302)

10. Analyze the results: on the first pass, examine Showplan results looking for table scans and total index usage. If an index is not used by any source code, simply delete it. Extra indexes are extra work for inserts, updates and deletes. At a minimum, mark these indexes for deletion and discuss them with other developers. If you find table scans, look for two possible causes:
    - Lack of an appropriate index. Research and see if there is any way to use or extend a current index.
    - The need for a new index. Consider wisely: Too many indexes on a table can be just as bad as not enough.

11. Analyze the results. On the second pass, examine the Showplan results comparing the logical I/O to the physical I/O. This comparison can point out a variety of problems. For example, compare how many actual

records you selected verses how many physical I/Os were generated. They should be mathematically justifiable. See Figure 5.2.

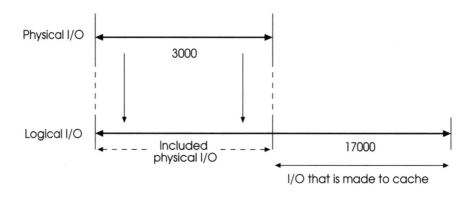

Total Logical I/O will be the combined physical and non cache-driven I/O. In this case 20,000 total I/O.

Figure 5.2
Logical vs. Physical I/O

WARNING
If the Logical I/O seems inordinately high check the code for efficency.
---

12. Balance the effect that too many indexes has upon insert, delete, and update performance.   Combine indexes if possible, and drop the least useful indexes.

5.7 The Dichotomy of Relational Design and Sybase Indexing

Relational database design involves referential integrity between associated entities. The natural affinity that an entity has with other entities (sometimes expressed as a Base Entity with Associative and Characteristic Entities) is managed and protected by indexes in Sybase. The 2K page granularity enables the system to optimize affinity. Related rows are usually located on the same index page, so the chances are high that all rows required for the search load into memory together. The 2K unit of measure chosen by Sybase therefore offers some advantages in dealing with indexes.

However, there is one particular problem presented by the 2K page size that continues to frustrate database designers. Many entities have primary keys that end in monotonically increasing values. This situation occurs in both large and small databases. In addition, these primary keys migrate by design into foreign key positions of the base entity's characteristic entities. This naturally occurring phenomenon is the proper expression of relational modeling.

Because Sybase uses the 2K page locking strategy, concurrency becomes a problem. Monotonic data is always inserted on the last page, in a manner similar to a heap structure, and locking occurs with query access. Despite these difficulties, System XI has done several things that help to overcome this apparent dichotomy. See the locking chapter for more information. See also Sybase's white paper entitled, "How Surrogate Primary Key Generation Affects Concurrency and the Cache Hit Ratio." Currently this white paper can be found on Compuserve's Sybase forum.

TABLE LOCKING AND CONCURRENCY CONTROLS

6

This chapter introduces locking, and illustrates how Sybase SQL Server handles locks. Using the information presented in this chapter, the SQL developer can apply good programming principles to maximize concurrency and minimize locking contention. In addition, the designer can place objects in optimal locations to minimize locking problems. Table locking is Sybase's concurrency control mechanism. The goal is to maximize concurrency and minimize access contention on tables being held by locks.

6.1 Consistency vs. Concurrency

A transaction is a logical unit of work. It is the mechanism that allows a programmer to combine two or more statements so that they behave like one statement. In order for transactions to work properly, Sybase must keep the data manipulated within the transaction consistent for the duration of the transaction. The rows manipulated by the transaction must not be changed by other users or processes for the duration of the transaction. For instance, if you are in the process of changing the sales price of an item, you don't want another user changing the sales price of the same item at the same time.

Database management systems ensure data consistency through a mechanism called *locking*. The locking process prevents user transactions from interfering with one another, guaranteeing that data will remain consistent within a transaction. Because locking is largely invisible to the programmer, and because locking has the effect of serializing users, the locking process has the potential to cause performance problems. In a large database with thousands of concurrent users and processes, locking can keep hundreds of users waiting while one user updates a specific page. If those hundreds of users are forced to wait for very long, they are going to complain. Your goal as a performance tuner is to minimize or eliminate contention between simultaneous users. The primary goal of the tuner is to provide a high level of consistency while maintaining an acceptable level of concurrency.

Sybase employs page level locking in almost all situations, although table locking is also used. If a transaction updates one row on a data page, and that data page contains nine other rows, all 10 rows are locked until that transaction releases the lock. There is currently much controversy in the industry about page level vs. row level locking. Smaller locks allow for greater concurrency but increase processing overhead.

6.2 Sybase Lock Types

Sybase uses two types of locks: shared and exclusive. The following sections describe these two locks and explain their differences.

6.2.1   Shared Lock

A *shared lock* is a read lock, taken when a process reads a page of data. Shared locks prevent writers from changing the data while the shared lock is active, but they allow other readers. When a shared lock is applied to a page, other transactions are also allowed to obtain a shared lock, but a transaction wanting to modify data on that page must wait.

Shared locks are released immediately after the page is no longer needed within a transaction. Use HOLDLOCK if it is absolutely necessary to hold the shared lock until the end of the transaction. It ensures read consistency throughout the entire transaction.

The syntax for HOLDLOCK is:

```
select selectlist
from tablename holdlock
```

For example, if an application shows a user the price of an item in inventory, the application may need to guarantee that the price does not change in

the time interval between the initial display of the price and the initiation of a
sale. HOLDLOCK keeps the lock active until a COMMIT TRANSACTION
or ROLLBACK is applied. Unfortunately, HOLDLOCK will block any users
or processes that need to change the price of the item. You should therefore use
HOLDLOCK very sparingly, and design applications so that the need for
HOLDLOCK is eliminated. Performance problems for locked users almost always result from the use of HOLDLOCK.

6.2.2   Exclusive Lock

An exclusive lock is a write lock, applied when a process changes the data
in an insert, update or delete operation. See Figure 6.1. No other reader processes or writer processes access data while an exclusive lock is active. Unlike
shared locks, exclusive locks are automatically applied for the length of a transaction. Therefore, long transactions have the potential to lock many reading or
writing processes for a long period of time. An example is shown below.

```
Process 1                           Process 2
begin tran
insert update grade
   set grade='A'                     select grade from grade
   where                               where class_id=1234
   student_id=8888888888
   and class_id=1234
commit tran
```

Assume that there is a clustered index on the grade table, on class_id. This
means that the INSERT in Process 1 is holding an exclusive lock on a page that
the SELECT statement in Process 2 wants to read. Since the transaction containing the INSERT starts first in this example, the exclusive lock is in effect
when the SELECT statement starts execution. Therefore, the SELECT statement must wait for the INSERT to finish and the COMMIT TRAN to execute
before it can proceed.

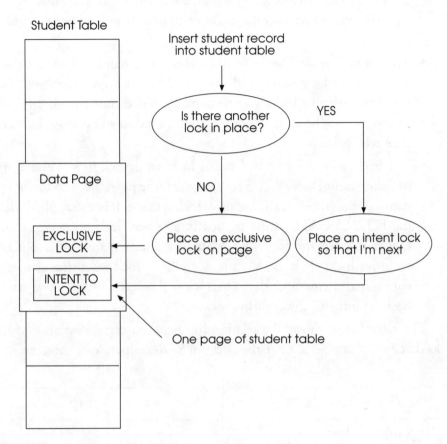

Figure 6.1
Locking for Inserts

Exclusive locks are blocked by read locks. This means that if there is a shared lock on the page, a process trying to write on that page has to wait until all shared locks have been released before it can obtain the exclusive lock. In the example above, if Process 2 began first, Process 1 would have to wait until the shared lock was released on the page that the insert process needed. There are three lock management mechanisms that Sybase uses as required to control exceptional situations. Each comes into play only after Sybase determines that the locking situation can exhaust its tracking abilities.

- The livelock: Since read locks have a higher priority, an exclusive lock could be blocked indefinitely by multiple readers continuously applying shared locks to a page. This problem is known as *starvation.* Sybase uses a livelock to wait until four different read locks have been completed.

- The demand lock: The Server then issues a demand lock on the page. The demand lock waits until the current locks are released and then takes an exclusive lock. The demand lock does not permit any new shared locks to be applied until it is promoted to an exclusive lock and then released.

- The update lock: Like the demand lock, an update lock is also a preliminary exclusive lock. It is applied when the pages are read for an update statement, before the exclusive lock is taken. It is also applied when the FOR UPDATE clause is used in a cursor declaration statement. Unlike the demand lock, an update lock allows shared locks, but not exclusive locks. It is escalated to a exclusive lock when the change is committed. Remember that a livelock will be taken if the server has to wait too long for the exclusive lock.

The table below shows the relationship between certain events and the locks that Sybase applies. Notice the effect of SARGs upon lock choices.

	Table Lock	Page Lock
Select using index	I,S	S
Select using index, holdlock	I,S	S
Select, no index used, no holdlock	I,S	S
Select, no index used, with hold-lock *[see Note 1]*	S	none
Insert	I,X	X
Update using SARG & useful index	I,X	U,X

Table 6.1
Locking Summary. I = intent lock, S = shared lock, X = exclusive lock, and U = update lock (Page 1 of 2)

	Table Lock	Page Lock
Update with no SARG, no index	X	none
Delete using SARG & useful index	I,X	X
Delete with no SARG, no index	X	none
Create clustered index	X	none
Create non-clustered index	S	none

Table 6.1
Locking Summary. I = intent lock, S = shared lock, X = exclusive lock, and U = update lock (Page 2 of 2)

Note 1. Lock appears the same but affects many more pages because a table scan is used until the row is found.

6.3 Deadlocks

Update, demand and live locks help to avoid deadlocks. A deadlock occurs when two or more processes hold locks on resources simultaneously needed by the others.

The classic example of deadlock involves the transfer of funds from a one account to another. In the code, the withdrawal logically occurs first. Deadlock results when one process withdraws money from the checking account (acquiring an exclusive lock) with the intent of depositing it into savings. If at the same time another process is withdrawing money from a savings account it will also acquire an exclusive lock on a page in the savings account table. If, when the first process tries to acquire a lock on the needed page in the savings account table the second process holds a lock, the first process will wait. If at the same time, the second process needs to deposit its money into the checking account and the first process holds a lock, it will wait as well. It may seem unlikely that such a thing can occur, because it is unlikely that a single bank customer would ever want to transfer money in two directions simultaneously. However, Sybase's use of page locking can cause this situation to arise unexpectedly because two or more customers can reside on the same page.

The code causing this deadlock is shown below. Let's assume that there is a clustered index on both tables on acct_no, and these two accounts are on the same data page. Both customers have the same account number for checking and savings.

```
Process 1                          Process 2
begin tran                         begin tran
update checking                    update savings
   set balance=balance-$100           set balance=balance-$1000
   where acct_no=1234                  where acct_no=1235
update savings                     update checking
   set balance=balance+$100           set balance=balance+$1000
   where acct_no=1234                  where acct_no=1235
commit tran                        commit tran
```

Deadlocks are also common when an application uses sequential keys and two processes are trying to insert at once. This situation arises in a heap table, or in a table with a clustered index on a sequential key. All inserts occur at the end of the table in both situations.

As another example, imagine a timesheet application which tracks all timesheets submitted by engineers. The engineers work on different projects. There is either a clustered index on timesheet id, which is a custom generated monotonic key (created before IDENTITY columns), or no clustered index at all, which means the table is a heap. In either case, there is a "hot spot" for insert activity, since all inserts occur at the end of the table.

```
Process 1                          Process 2
begin tran
select @max=                       begin tran
   max(timesheet_id)               select @max=
   from timesheet holdlock            max(timesheet_id)
insert into timesheet                 from timesheet holdlock
   (timesheet_id, column_list)    insert into timesheet
   values                            (timesheet_id, column_list)
   (@max, values_list)               values
commit tran                           (@max, values_list)
                                   commit tran
```

In the example above, the first process takes a shared lock on the table to get the max, and keeps the lock for the duration of the transaction. The other process also takes a shared lock on the table for the duration of the transaction. In the meantime, the first process wants to perform the insert. However, the first process has a shared lock on the whole table, preventing the first process from escalating its lock. Since the second process also wants to escalate its lock and cannot, the two processes deadlock.

Uncontrolled, deadlocks can create severe and often hidden performance problems. Sybase can detect deadlocks and resolves them by terminating the younger of the two deadlocked processes. In properly written code, the terminated process can decide its own fate. Your code should be prepared for deadlocks and handle them appropriately. For example, it can re-execute to complete its task. The code may appear to work correctly but it will be extremely slow because of the cost of detecting the deadlock, killing the process and then restarting it. You therefore want to prevent deadlocks in your code and you also want your DBAs to frequently check error logs and sp_lock to find deadlocks that are occurring invisibly in your system.

If you always access the tables in alphabetical order, you will avoid the checking/savings account problem illustrated above. The natural thing to do when performing a transfer of money (at least if you are a bank) is to perform the subtraction operation first. However, if you follow the alphabetical order rule and you want to code the transfer of money from savings to checking, you would add the money to the checking account first and then subtract it from the savings because "C" comes before "S." Following this simple rule will prevent a large portion of all possible deadlocks.

Here are some tips that help you avoid deadlock with sequential keys:

- Use the IDENTITY column instead of trying to maintain your own algorithm with incrementing a sequential key. Keep in mind that use of IDENTITY can cause loss of numbers if your system crashes frequently. IDENTITY will grab a range of numbers and hold them in memory. These numbers disappear if the system terminates ungracefully
- Use a clustered index on fields other than sequential fields
- Use a partitioned heap table to spread out the inserts
- To avoid deadlock with two or more table accesses
  - Always access the tables in a specified order

- Always access tables in alphabetical order
- Avoid table locks in long running transactions

6.4 Checking For Deadlocks

Sybase can detect and resolve deadlocks automatically. If a deadlock is found, the process with the least amount of CPU time becomes the "victim," and the transaction belonging to this process is rolled back. You detect this behavior by capturing the 1205 message in your client application code, and should resubmit the transaction. Your code should not resubmit a transaction indiscriminately, however. It should resubmit some fixed number of times and then report the error to the user in some way.

In all releases prior to System XI, deadlock checking was initiated immediately when a process waited for a lock. For processes that are not deadlocked, this mandatory checking consumes unnecessary CPU time. In System XI, deadlock checking is deferred by default. The server waits 500 milliseconds after the process begins to wait, and then checks for a deadlock condition. In System XI, the length of time the server waits before performing deadlock checking is tunable, in milliseconds. Use sp_configure deadlock checking period (a DBA function) to tune this number to be higher for systems where deadlocks occur very infrequently. Deadlock checking is a server-wide configuration variable.

You should trap for 1205 messages in any code that modifies data.

6.5 Lock Escalation

Sybase can upgrade page level table level locks in a process called lock escalation. Escalation occurs automatically under certain specific conditions. In any process needing to hold a large number of page locks, you can improve performance if the process can hold one table lock instead.

By default, escalation results when the SQL Server determines that more a process needs to hold 200 or more page locks. For example:

```
update student
set tuition = 1800
```

This statement escalates to a table lock when Sybase realizes that the whole table needs updating.

When possible, improve the selectivity of a transaction by adding a WHERE clause. For example, update the tuition for a specific SID. This is especially important for updates and deletes because they result in exclusive locks, which do not allow concurrent readers.

6.6 Table Locks

An intent lock is a table lock that keeps track of page locks for that table. Intent locks do not actually lock the table; they supply internal information concerning locks active for the table.

There are two kinds of intent locks: shared and exclusive. An exclusive table lock does not allow any access to the entire table for the duration of the transaction. An exclusive table lock is applied when a page lock has escalated to a table lock for a write operation.

A shared table lock functions the same way that a shared page lock does: It locks writers but allows other readers on the whole table rather than just a page. A shared table lock prohibits an exclusive table lock or any exclusive page lock from being applied to the table or its pages.

A shared table lock is applied when a page lock has escalated to a table lock for a read.

6.6.1 When Table Locks are Applied

There are conditions other than escalation that cause Sybase to apply table level locks. For example, shared table locks are applied when the query has the following characteristics:
- When there is no index that can be used, and if a HOLDLOCK is used.
- When an OR clause is used (the query must do a table scan).
- When 200 pages have been locked, SQL Server will escalate it to one shared table lock.
- When a table scan is determined necessary for a read operation (such as no WHERE clause specified).
- When a nonclustered index is created.

Exclusive Table Locks are applied:
- When a clustered index is created.
- When no index can be used for an Update or Delete operation.

- When 200 pages have an exclusive lock, SQL Server will escalate it to one exclusive page lock.
- When a table scan is mandated for an Update or Delete operation (such as Truncate Table or no WHERE clause specified).

6.6.2   Lock Compatibility

Shared locks are compatible with other shared locks and update locks. Exclusive locks are not compatible with any other locks. Lock escalation cannot occur if there is a conflict with any existing lock.

This incompatibility can cause problems. If there is one exclusive page lock active for a period of time in one process and a reading process has more than 200 locks, it cannot escalate to a table lock. Such a situation can lead to the reader acquiring a huge number of locks, until all available locks have been exhausted. Your code should not hold locks (especially exclusive locks) longer than absolutely necessary.

You can detect the number of locks held by using sp_lock. If you find that reading processes are acquiring an excessive number of locks because of the existence of an exclusive lock, you can increase the maximum number of locks allowed on the specific server. Remember, you may also have to increase the overall memory size, because locks consume memory at a rate of 72 bytes per lock. While you will still have performance problems, the application will run.

6.6.3   Lock Promotion Thresholds

System XI allows the DBA and SQL developer more control over lock escalations. For example, use sp_setpglockpromote to allow table locks to happen more or less frequently as desired. Lock promotion thresholds can be set for a specific table, database or server.

There are three thresholds that you can customize:
- High Water Mark (HWM)
- Low Water Mark (LWM)
- Percent (PCT)

Syntax:

```
sp_setpglockpromote "server" "database" or "table",
"objectname", LWM, HWM, PCT
```

Example:

```
sp_setpglockpromote "table", "student", 200, 1000, 70
```

Here is an explanation of the above command: If the number of locks held on the STUDENT table falls between the low water mark (200) and the high water mark (1000) and the percentage of locks held is 70% of the number of pages in the whole table, then Sybase will acquire a table level lock. If the number of locks is below the low water mark, then Sybase will use only page level locks. If the number of locks is above the high water mark, then Sybase will automatically use table level locks.

You will probably find that the default behavior (200 page locks forces table locks) is sufficient for most situations. However, with large tables you may want to change the percentage and/or increase the low water mark: if 20% of the table is locked, force promotion, for instance. As you tinker with these values, ABSOLUTELY make sure you have increased the total number of available locks on the server with sp_configure, especially if you are increasing the low water mark and allowing more page level locks per table.

For large tables, you should modify lock promotion thresholds. 200 pages is a very small percent of a very large table. For instance, 200 pages locked for a table with 200,000 rows is only 0.1% of the table. It is unlikely that you want to force escalation in this case. Set LWM and HWM to larger values for large tables.

In order to use sp_setpglockpromote effectively, you must have knowledge of the space used by the table. Use the sp_spaceused command to determine space consumption. For example:

```
sp_spaceused "tuition"
name                    rowtotal    reserved        data
    index_size          unused

---------------    ----------   -------------   -------------
    ---------------    ---------------

tuition                 2000014     61552 KB        61540 KB
    0 KB                12 KB
(return status = 0)
```

Monitor the locks periodically to see how many locks are used for large, heavily accessed tables. (Run sp_lock, discussed later in this chapter). If too many locks are held by one process, consider changing these lock promotion thresholds.

6.7 Lock Isolation Levels

The ANSI standard SQL specifies 4 levels of locking isolation.

Level	Name	Description	Sybase Enforced
0	Dirty Read	A transaction can read a row that has been changed by another process but may not have been committed yet. If the transaction is rolled back, then the original data read would be wrong.	set command (the table must have a unique index or the database must be read only)
1	Committed Read	A transaction cannot modify data that is being read.	Sybase enforces this by default
2	Cursor Stability (ladder locking)	A transaction reads a row and the shared lock is held until the next row is requested.	Sybase enforces this by enforcing level 3
3	Repeatable Reads (serializable) No Phantoms	If a transaction queries data by using a WHERE clause criteria, the result set is guaranteed to be the same for the duration of the transaction. No one can update a row that makes it ineligible to meet the query criteria for the duration of the transaction.	holdlock

Table 6.2
Lock Isolation Levels

If a transaction queries data using WHERE clause criteria, the result set is guaranteed to be the same for the duration of the transaction. No one can update a row that makes it ineligible to meet the query criteria. This restriction applies for the duration of the transaction.

Note that Sybase does not support level 2 by itself. Sybase says they support level 2 as part of level 3, but the strict definition of level 2 does not hold locks as long as level 3. In Sybase, moving to a new row that falls on another page causes the lock to release on the previous page. In level 3, the shared lock should be held for the first page for the duration of the transaction.

Sybase has not supported cursors for very long, and this may be the reason for the lack of level 2 support. Cursor features in Sybase are not as mature as those for other DBMS products such as Oracle and Informix, who have supported cursors for many years. For instance, other database products support scrollable cursors able fetch forward, backward, relatively, and so on, while Sybase does not. Cursors are de-emphasized in Sybase primarily because they do not support set theory, which is essential to the relational model from a theorist's point of view. More importantly, from a client/server practitioner's point of view cursors generate network traffic. Cursors are therefore more effective in stored procedures.

Another reason for lack of support for isolation level 2 is Sybase's page level locking strategy. Level 2 seems to assume the use of row level locking. As the cursor moves from row to row, Level 2 assumes the release of locks on the last row and the taking of locks on the next row.

6.7.1   Changing Isolation Levels

The default isolation level for Sybase is 1. Note that the ANSI standard states it should be level 0, which allows dirty reads. You can set the isolation level to a different value in four different ways, based on its scope.

To change the level of isolation for a specific select statement:

- Use HOLDLOCK to set to level 3.
- Use the AT ISOLATION clause to set to 0, 1 or 3.
- Use the READ UNCOMMITTED clause to set to 0.

To change the level of isolation for the entire session or transaction use SET TRANSACTION ISOLATION LEVEL to 0, 1 or 3.

The locking level can be retrieved with the select @@isolation statement.

> **HINT**
> Use noholdlock if a high level of isolation is used (3) and the shared locks
> are not needed until transaction completion. When using level 3 isola-
> tion, use noholdlock whenever possible.

When used with chained mode, the isolation level is in force for all statements that imply "begin transaction," including select statements. This means
that if level 3 is used, locks are held until the next "commit" is encountered.
Use chained mode only when absolutely required, and only when all developers
are appropriately trained in its use and in minimizing locking.

6.8 Chained Transactions

Chained transactions are extremely dangerous. You should never use them
in Sybase databases.

The Sybase SQL Server has always operated on the principle of small
transactions, including using the "singleton transaction" default behavior. Singleton behavior means that SQL Server assumes that every statement forms its
own implicit "begin transaction" and "commit work" boundaries. Every statement is therefore treated as a "singleton" transaction (a transaction consisting
of one statement), unless explicit "begin transaction/commit work" logic is
used at a higher level.

However, the ANSI SQL standard works differently, and states that every
statement which either reads or changes data—including the SELECT statement—implicitly opens a transaction and must be explicitly committed with
the "commit work" boundary. This is called a "chained transaction." Every
statement is chained together into one transaction by default, until a "COM-
MIT WORK" is encountered.

In chained mode, a select statement will hold a shared lock until it encounters a commit. Developers may not realize that just about ANY statement
will hold locks and keep a transaction open until a COMMIT is found. Here
are the statements which open a transaction in COMMIT mode:
- select
- update
- delete

- insert
- open (for cursors)
- fetch (for cursors)

Note that any SELECT statement will open a transaction, even one which assigns a variable to a value.

Chained transactions are supported in SQL Server version 10 and above, and must be explicitly set at the beginning of the session with the "set chained on" statement. The "set chained on" statement is active for the duration of the session, unless it is set to "off" later in the session (a practice which is to be strictly avoided. Do not mix modes.) You can find out which mode is currently in use by selecting the global variable @@tranchained: 0 means unchained and 1 means chained.

WARNING
NEVER set chained on in the middle of a session. Use it consistently.

It is vital that programmers agree on a chaining policy and set a standard before any code is written. The authors strongly recommend that you use Sybase's default, unless portability is important. If there is a chance that the same code will be running against heterogeneous database products, you should probably have everyone agree to use chained transactions, and then use COMMIT statements frequently.

HINT
A developer should be assigned to proof the code and verify that there are frequent "commits" in code utilizing chained transactions.

Chained transactions can hold locks for the duration of the session, and if no "commit" is encountered they will only be released when the session terminates. This is especially common in isql. The user usually is not aware of the locks, and the performance degradation due to the locks can be severe. This problem is also extremely acute at higher levels of isolation, such as level 3. See the section on isolation.

Transactions behave totally differently in chained vs. unchained modes. Consider the following code:

```
insert into student (student_id, first_name, last_name,
    date_of_birth)
values (9090109090, 'John', 'Smith', '02/02/58')
begin tran
insert into grade (class_id, student_id) values
    (123, 9090109090)
rollback tran
```

In the example above, if chained is set, the rollback would rollback to the beginning. This means that no inserts are done at all. If Sybase's default of unchained is in effect, the rollback only affects the insert into the grade table, which means that the student information gets inserted correctly. Each mode works off of different assumptions, and completely different results occur. This is why you NEVER mix chained and unchained modes in one application. Decide on a policy and use it consistently throughout the application.

Remember that you should never require user interaction in the middle of a transaction. You should encapsulate all transactions in stored procedures. You should call a stored procedure and pass parameters to activate a transaction.

WARNING
Many front end application builders, such as Powerbuilder, automatically enforce chained transactions. There is an AUTOCOMMIT feature which you can set to turn chaining off.

6.9 Viewing Locks

To obtain information about locks currently held and processes blocked, you can use sp_lock and sp_who. On Compuserve in the Sybase forum's library, you can obtain two extensions to sp_lock: sp_lock_what, which includes the name of the table involved, and sp_block, which lists only locks blocking other processes.

You can specify a process id, and sp_lock will display only those locks for that process. Without a process id, sp_lock displays all locks.

6.9.1   Table locks

As an example of the use of sp_lock, imagine that a query performs a select without a WHERE clause. This will cause a table scan. Below is the output of the sp_lock command in this situation.

```
1> sp_lock
2> go
spid  locktype   table_id    page  dbname  class

6     Sh_intent 384004399  0      college Non Cursor Lock
1     Sh_table  16003088   0      college Non Cursor Lock
```

A select statement sets a shared lock. The Sh_table lock shown is a shared table lock indicating that a table scan was needed.

6.9.2   Page locks

Another query performs a select with a WHERE clause on a table that has an index on the field referenced in the WHERE clause. Using a comparison operator on an indexed column limits the scope of the lock.

Here's the output of sp_lock:

```
1> sp_lock
2> go
spid  locktype   table_id    page  dbname  class

7     Sh_intent 16003088   0      college Non Cursor Lock
7     Sh_page   16003088   416    college Non Cursor Lock
```

Remember that the Sh_intent lock is the informational lock, providing information about what locks are applied to anything in the table. The Sh_page lock is applied in this example instead of the table lock because of the index.

6.10 Blocked Processes

A query performs a select with a WHERE clause which uses an index. While this query is running, another process tries to perform an update. Here is what sp_lock will show:

```
1> sp_lock
2> go
spid  locktype       table_id page dbname  class

----  --------       -------- ---- ------  -----------
7     Sh_intent      16003088 0    college Non Cursor Lock
7     Sh_page-blk    16003088 416  college Non Cursor Lock
8     Ex_intent      16003088 0    college Non Cursor Lock
8     Update_page    16003088 416  college Non Cursor Lock
```

The suffix "-blk" indicates that this lock is blocking another process.

The Ex_intent lock signifies that a write lock wants to execute, but since it's blocked, the Update_page lock is set as an intermediate lock.

You can also use sp_who to examine blocked processes. The status of the blocked process is indicated as "lock sleep." The blk value will indicate the process id of the lock blocking it.

6.11 Heap Tables and Lock Contention

Heap tables are tables with no clustered index. They are more susceptible to lock contention than tables with clustered indexes because inserts occur at the end of the last data page. Many users inserting into the same table at the same time would block each other.

Use of the proper clustered index would spread out the inserted pages. However, a clustered index on a monotonic (serially increasing) key would still cause a locking bottleneck at the last page.

Use of the new partition feature for heaps is one way you can avoid this problem (see the design chapter). If this option is not available, consider the following alternatives.

6.11.1   Rows per Page to Reduce Lock Contention

Limiting rows per page in a heap table can improve performance by reducing contention. Lowering the number of rows per page reduces the probability that the page you need contains a row that another user needs at the same time. Be aware that reducing rows per page does not solve the insert bottleneck. Instead it solves the retrieval problem by spreading queries and inserts out over different parts of the table.

There are two ways to adjust the number of records stored on a page:

- fillfactor
- max_rows_per_page value for a table

6.11.2 Fillfactor: an Initial Lock Contention Fighter

Fillfactor is effective for a table that will be loaded into an empty structure, i.e. before data is loaded into a table or clustered index structure. Fillfactor allows you to specify how much of the page is filled. For example, a fillfactor of 80 leaves 20% of the page empty.

Fillfactor can be especially beneficial for clustered indexes. Clustered indexes store the data in the leaf node of the index, in the order specified by the index. When the server tries to insert a new row somewhere on a page and there is no more room the page will split in half, moving half the rows to the new page. This causes several locks while the server realigns the index page pointers. The page being split is locked, along with the rest of the branch of the clustered index structure. This is obviously I/O and lock intensive, and you want to avoid this if possible. Page splitting can frequently cause more contention than a regular insert on the same page. For tables expecting heavy insert activity, you want to leave more free space on each page to accommodate new rows being added and to avoid page splits.

However, the server does not maintain the fillfactor over time. As new rows are inserted, free space will obviously decline. Therefore, the two main advantages of fillfactor (reduced rows on a page and reduced page splits) will go away. Fillfactor is only a temporary advantage unless you reassert the fillfactor at regular intervals.

To determine the proper fillfactor, do some simple math. Make sure any fillfactor you use leaves enough room for at least one new row per page. Otherwise fillfactor is a waste of time and space. Sybase uses 32 bytes of overhead on a data page. Therefore, a page has 2016 bytes of usable space. To calculate how many rows can fit on a page, use the size of the row plus row overhead (at least four bytes) and divide 2016 by row size. Refer to Chapter 5 in the System XI Performance and Tuning Guide for a detailed discussion of how to calculate exact row size. Remember that nullable fields and variable length fields consume extra space in Sybase. When a page split occurs, 50% of the rows from the page being split are moved to the new page and 50% remain on the old page. This is essentially a 50% fillfactor, if you want to think of it in those terms.

6.11.3   Maximum Rows per Page and Lock Contention

System XI allows you to specify the maximum number of rows per page. By reducing rows per page you reduce contention. The irony in using max rows per page, however, is it may increase the frequency of page splits, as opposed to fillfactor reducing them. Because there are less rows allowed on a page, the page will "fill up" faster, and therefore have to split sooner than a more densely populated page.

Although Sybase does not yet support row level locking, max rows per page is a way to approximate it. If you have the disk space, you can specify max_rows_per_page=1 and produce the same effect as row level locking. Space consumption would be high however. Specifying a lower number for max rows per page reduces contention because there are fewer rows on a page, and fewer possibilities of two or more processes needing the same page.

Max rows per page is specified by using the create table, create index, alter table, or sp_chattribute commands. Like fillfactor, you should use it on an empty table or index for best results. If used on a table with existing data, it would not reorganize data that has already been loaded; it will only affect new data.

6.11.4   Using Max Rows per Page to Reduce Contention

Max rows per page works on index leaf pages (both clustered and nonclustered) and data pages. The syntax for the option is as follows:

```
create table subject(col1 datatype,col2 datatype...)

    with max_rows_per_page=5
```

Use sp_chgattribute or alter table to change an existing table's max rows per page. These procedures will not affect data already existing in the table. In order to reorganize existing data you can create a clustered index (or drop and recreate it, if the table already has one) or bulk copy the data out, wipe the data from the table with the truncate command and then bulk copy the data back in again.

6.11.5   An Example

This example shows the effect of max_rows_per_page set to a value of two. It is purposely set very small so you can see the large number of pages allocated. The table has only two columns: an identity column and a varchar field.

```
select * from subject
go
col1      col2

-------- -------------------------------
       1 blah
       2 yikes
       3 so what
       4 go to it
       5 go for it
       6 la la land
(6 rows affected)


sp_spaceused subject
go
name                    rowtotal   reserved        data
     index_size         unused

---------------- ---------- -------------- --------------

---------------- ----------------
subject                 6          16 KB         6 KB
     0 KB              10 KB
(return status = 0)
```

As you can see, there are only six small rows in the table, yet three pages are used for a total of 6K bytes of allocated space. Be prepared to waste disk space when you use this feature. However, the technique can often pay off in high performance because it allows concurrency.

6.11.6   How Cursors Affect Locks

Read-only cursors hold a shared lock for the page containing the current cursor position. An interesting phenomenon arises when an update occurs while a cursor is reading on another page. If the table is a heap, all inserts occur on the last page with the exception of partitioned tables. If the current position of the cursor is located on any other page when an insert occurs, the cursor will read the new insert even though the new row was not there when it began reading.

To avoid this problem, always use "set close on endtran" in all sessions which use transactions and cursors. This step will automatically close any open cursors at the end of every transaction, and therefore release any active locks. If you do not do this, a cursor can remain open accidentally and hold locks for the duration of the session, leading to dramatic performance degradation.

SYSTEM X / SYSTEM XI
Reduce rows per page by either using max_rows_per_page or fillfactor to reduce lock contention that may be caused by cursors.

6.12 Concurrency Analysis

The authors recommend that you perform concurrency analysis, which studies the interaction and possible conflicts between users, in advance, before any code is written. Concurrency analysis maps out the likelihood that multiple users will be performing the same or conflicting operations on the same data at once.

Perform execution thread analysis and create a transaction map which ties the following items together:

- Business transactions
- Data elements
- Business Rules
- Time of day

Next, write down the high activity areas of contention, and their characteristics:

- Numerous queries on the same data, but a low number of updates or inserts
- Numerous inserts interfering with many queries
- Numerous inserts interfering with each other

See the chapter on execution thread analysis for a detailed step by step description of how to perform this analysis.

TRANSACTION DESIGN SOLUTIONS

Regardless of the source of contention, make the size of transactions as small as possible without damaging business integrity. Double check against business rules. When an update or delete statement indicates a range in the WHERE clause, keep the range as small as possible. Very large ranges may need many data pages to resolve the query. They will either lock many pages or will force a table scan and lock the entire table.

6.13 Optimistic Locking

It is absolutely essential that you keep user interaction out of transaction processing. You should use transactions only in the context of a stored procedure. There are no exceptions to this rule. Optimistic locking using timestamp comparisons is a strategy you can use to handle user interaction without putting it in a transaction.

Sybase by default uses pessimistic locking. It assumes that someone will perform a write when a read is taking place. In order to accommodate this assumption, Sybase holds locks on all data being read. The opposite approach is to assume that no writes will probably occur when the read is taking place. So no lock is held. Instead, when a row is modified, the time that the event was performed is recorded in a special timestamp field.

When a process reads a row, it records the time that the read takes place. When the process that performs a read wants to modify the data later, it examines the last modified timestamp and compares it with the time it read the row. If the row has been modified since the last read took place, it does not allow the update. However, if the row has not been modified since the read, the update is allowed.

Sybase's browse mode allows user interaction without locks. The table must be created with a special timestamp column. The syntax follows:

```
create table class_list

(student_id int,class_id int,gradechar(5),timestamp)
```

Notice that the timestamp column does not get a regular name or datatype. The "timestamp" identifier is a name and datatype rolled into one.

An existing table can be retrofitted with a timestamp column:

```
alter table Payment add timestamp
```

When the timestamp column is added to an existing table, NULL is placed in the column for each existing record. To generate an initial timestamp value for all rows in the table, use update with the column's value:

```
update tuition set tuition_amt= tuition_amt
```

To use the timestamp column when doing a select statement and not hold locks, use the FOR BROWSE option in your front end application's select statement:

```
select tuition_amt, quarter, calendar_year
      from tuition t, student s
   where t.student_id = s.student_id
   for browse
```

Use the tsequal() function (or a simple variable/column comparison) to compare the timestamp for when it was read to the stored value in the update or delete statement:

```
update payment set payment_amt=@newamt
   where receipt_nbr=@receipt
   and tsequal(timestamp, @ts)
```

In the example above, this code appears in a stored procedure which is passed the parameters @receipt, @newamt and @ts from the client application such as Powerbuilder.

In the initial select for browse, the column names are assigned local variables in the application, including the timestamp, and the latter is not displayed to the user. Timestamp must be declared as a binary(8) or varbinary datatype; verify that your front end software supports this datatype.

6.14 Locking Strategies

Locking provides a mechanism for data integrity, but has a side effect of sometimes restricting concurrency. We want to create an environment of optimum concurrency: Our objective is to balance the competing needs of concurrency and integrity to yield maximum performance. The onus is on the developer to understand the restrictions imposed by the Sybase locking mechanisms and code to them.

To achieve these objectives we consider three approaches. The first is valuable during transaction analysis and development. The second benefits the development of index strategies. The third revolves around structural considerations.

6.14.1   Locking Strategies during Transaction Analysis and Development

When considering a transaction keep the following points in mind:

- **Where possible and logical use dirty reads and browse mode.** The advantage of dirty reads is that they allow the maximum possible concurrent access to a table, short of applying no lock at all. It allows multiple reads on the same data, and also allows writing while others are holding the data mid-transaction.

- **Avoid the use of holdlocks and level 3 isolation** unless absolutely necessary. This level imposes the maximum restrictions on data use and effectively eliminates concurrency. This option completely serializes both readers and writers.

- **Within the body of a transaction consider using noholdlock** for SELECTs from tables in the middle of high isolation transactions where long locks are not necessary. By default a SELECT in a transaction will take a shared lock, and if the transaction does not require this lock it reduces concurrency needlessly. By specifying noholdlock you free the data for reuse by other transactions.

- **Do not ever put user interaction within the code for a transaction.** Transactions should complete as quickly as possible, and user interaction virtually guarantees exceedingly long transaction intervals. If the user leaves an operation unfinished, the locks prevent all other users from accessing that portion of the database. User interaction delays will bring the system to a complete standstill unless you keep them out of transactions.

- **Ensure shortest possible transactions:** During and after the development of transaction code, and during contiguous calls to multiple transactions, analyze the complete set of transactions to ensure that they are as short as possible.

- **If your transaction has cursors, always use "set close on endtran."** See the Sybase reference manual for details. If you forget this step, the cursor holds a lock indefinitely.

- **Remember to write a retry trap for deadlock victims** so that they have a chance to complete their work. Although said before it bears repeating: Keep transactions short. Long transactions that have to restart after deadlock termination will consume significant resources

By following these simple transaction development guidelines you will significantly help to maximize concurrency. You will also improve system scalability.

6.14.2   Locking Strategies during Index Analysis and Development

When considering the development of indexes, keep two things in mind to ensure high concurrency:

- **Use index coverage:** You can use indexes to avoid table scans and excessive locking contention. One particularly potent tool is index *coverage*. Index coverage uses a non-clustered index in which all of the data needed by the query is included in the index structure. With such an index, query access does not require physical access of the data table and eliminates all locks on the data table pages.

- **Avoid creating clustered indexes that include a monotonic data type** in the key. The monotonic data has the effect of turning the table into a heap table. See the index chapter for details. Use either a partitioned table or clustered index on a different kind of key.

6.14.3   Structural Considerations

Consider the following structural changes in databases suffering from poor concurrency:

- **Reduce the number of rows per 2K page.** This step improves concurrency at the expense of disk space.

- **Use fillfactor:** The initial use of fillfactor to avoid page splits provides a mechanism for you to give a performance boost to tables known to have a large amount of insert activity. The weakness of this strategy is that as soon as the fillfactor is filled the benefit disappears. The DBA must at some point rebuild the table with a new fill factor. By rebuilding during a low-load time of day you can improve inserts during peak load.

- **DBAs can help monitor system performance by regularly using sp_lock to view locks held,** especially during peak insertion and deletion times If the DBA notices deadlocks, too many locks being held, lock growth, etc., it will indicate that problems exist in the code. It would be easy to create a script that executes every 15 minutes to monitor for lock problems.

QUERY STRATEGIES

This chapter presents a number of general performance tuning strategies and acts as a prelude to the specific expression and operator tuning tactics presented in the next chapter. This list acts as a useful reference and checklist that allows you to verify that you have not forgotten anything in your search for better performance.

7.1 Use Showplan when Testing Code to Make Sure that the Optimizer uses Appropriate Indexes

The optimizer's choices may surprise you. By running Showplan, as described in the optimizer chapter, you can check on the optimizer's behavior.

7.2 Use "Set statistics time on" to Benchmark Performance

This facility automatically tracks CPU usage and lets you get accurate benchmark results. Use it before and after making performance-related changes to ensure that you have accomplished your goal.

7.3 Know the Essential Nature of your Data

It is extremely important to know not just the data's structure, but also the actual data values and how the business plans to use it. Data demographics (the distribution of the data) vary over time, and can have a tremendous effects on query processing.

For example, when a new database for a college goes into production the semester/year values will not be very selective. All values in the new database will reflect the current semester/year only. Over time, however, the combination of these two fields becomes more selective. The percentage of selectivity is important, as the optimizer evaluates which indexes to use based on the selectivity.

WARNING

Do not forget to update the statistics periodically so the optimizer can be properly informed about the selectivity of each column.

7.4 Pay Attention to Complex Queries and Subqueries

When queries become problematic, consider alternatives such as:
- including extra SARGs for increased selectivity in the WHERE clause
- using temp tables
- chopping the query length
- using other client-side solutions to maximize asynchronous processing

---

WARNING

In all versions of Sybase prior to system XI, the SARG is evaluated with left hand column preference. This is no longer the case with system XI. In System XI column-operator-expression and expression-operator-column are evaluated equally.

The following examples illustrate the value of adding an extra SARG:
Example 1:

```
use college
set Showplan on
select a.student_id_nbr
      ,a.last_name
      ,b.department_name
```

```
from student a
      ,department b
```
where a.major = b.department_code
  and a.major = "biol"

Example 2:
```
select a.student_id_nbr
       ,a.last_name
       ,b.department_name
  from student a
       ,department b
```
  where a.major = b.department_code
    and a.major = "biol"
    and b.department_code = "biol"

The first query uses a table scan, while the second query with the extra SARG uses the clustered index. While in this case the reason was artificially induced, there are many situations which will mysteriously come and go as data skew changes the optimizer's index decision. Including extra SARGs can help combat this type of problem.

7.5 Use Stored Procedures and Triggers when it Makes Sense to do so

Stored procedures and triggers improve performance. After their first execution Sybase stores their query plans in memory. At the next execution, all of the preliminary set-up steps are eliminated. This increases query response time substantially.

Stored procedures also decrease network traffic, because only the stored procedure name travels across the network, and only those rows needed get sent back.

Stored procedures and triggers offer a loose form of encapsulation or data independence. They help to separate database logic from application logic, and assist in the performance tuning process as a whole, because the query loses unnecessary overhead and the essential server processing can be optimized.

7.6 Always Start with a Normalized Design. Consider Denormalization ONLY after Normalized Design has been Proven Unsuccessful

A database must be normalized first to prevent data integrity anomalies from invading the performance tuning processes. You should always have a normalized design that you can return to if it becomes necessary. See the Design chapter for more information.

7.7 Consider a User's High-Level Business Rules with Regard to I/O Performance Tuning Issues

Obviously you should never compromise business rules for the sake of performance. However, you can often find a creative solution that accomplishes the objectives of a business rule while at the same time achieves performance gains. It is important to capture and refer to concrete rules for this process to be successful.

For example, if a transaction is too long you can sometimes segment it into smaller transactions so locks are not held and contention with other processes is minimized. In this case, it is very important to refer to the business rules so you can verify that they are properly enforced in the new transaction design.

Similarly, if the business requires a specific calculation, it may not matter when you perform the aggregation. You might:

- Store the aggregate in a master table maintained by a trigger
- Maintain a normalized data structure and perform the calculation on the fly when needed
- Perform the calculation in the front end tool on the client side

7.8 Perform Lock Analysis

Use lock analysis tools. If you do not have access to these tools, you can use sp_lock and SQL monitor to analyze lock contention. You can also build CRUD matrices (Create Read Update Delete) with the added lock information. See the chapter on locking for further details.

	Create Student	Enroll Student	Assign Class	Delete Class	Assign Teacher
Student	CU	R	R	U	-
Class	R	R	U	D	U
Teacher	R	R	R	U	U
Grade	-	-	-	U	-

Table 7.1
Example CRUD Matrix

7.9 Use Transaction Chopping Techniques

The smaller and faster the transaction is, the quicker the locks held by the access will be released.   In addition to releasing locks for concurrency, succinct and modular transactions provide logical design benefits such as reuse.

Maintain the integrity of the business rules throughout the transaction chopping process.

7.10 Review your Memory Layout with the DBA and System Administrator

You should work closely with the system administrator to carefully plan memory needs and memory layout. Disk I/O can be a large bottleneck in database applications, and the best way to minimize it is through the judicious use of memory. The general rule is "More is Better," so you want to have as much memory as possible allocated to SQL Server. You also want to use a dedicated hardware platform for the database server if at all possible. You don't want the server to have to compete with any other applications for resources, since DBMSs are extremely resource intensive.

7.11 Review the Hardware and Network Architecture

You need to have a base knowledge of your hardware and network limitations. For example: If your system administrator says, "We've got 10 disk drives. Don't worry!" but the 10 disk drives are working through one disk controller, you may have a problem and you might want to politely recommend that the company acquire more disk controllers. Knowledge of the hardware will allow you to make these recommendations.

> **NOTE**
> System XI offers additional physical tuning capabilities. See the memory chapter for further details. For example: it is advisable to place tempdb in memory. Sometimes, due to hardware constraints, it is advisable to place it on a RAM disk; however, in another case the OS and hardware architecture may dictate that a RAM drive utilizing a private named cache would be preferable.

7.12 Use Segmentation

Segmentation can be a powerful ally in placing or separating particularly hot tables. Spreading out a table over multiple disks and controllers allows for parallel reads and minimizes contention. You need to carefully monitor disk usage because when all the segments are full all processing will stop.

7.13 Separate Client/Server OTLP Systems and ad-hoc DSS (Decision Support System) Queries

This is a simple piece of advice, but you would be surprised at how often it is ignored. There is no systematic analysis that can provide you with a scalable OLTP system combined with an ad-hoc query (DSS) capability.   Even if you cannot afford to separate the decision support and OLTP environments completely, you can create a duplicate of a very high access, high volume table within the same database for decision support.

7.14 "Select into" is Fast. Use it as Often as Possible

"Select into" does not have a transaction log activity bottleneck associated with it. Therefore, use it to create tables based on other tables whenever possible. For example, instead of using the CREATE TABLE statement use "select into."

7.15 Perform Periodic Re-creation of Clustered Indexes with Fillfactor

Periodic re-creation of clustered indexes with the correct fillfactor in an insert intensive environment will improve performance. Fillfactor pads the data pages. When a new row is inserted a page split can be avoided, thereby reducing physical I/O. Recreate the indexes during a low-load time of the day to improve performance during peak loads.

7.16 Bring Down the Server and Bring it Back up Again Periodically to Clear Memory

Old query plans can clog memory because multiple copies of a stored procedure with different query plans can exist in memory at the same time. It is impossible to predict which query plan any given user might get when they execute the stored procedure. It is good practice to flush memory completely to eliminate old query plans based on inaccurate statistics. The only way you can flush memory is to bring down the server.

7.17 Re-analyze SQL Clauses per Execution Thread with the Most Experienced Staff Available

Choose queries that you will get the most "bang for the buck" (see the chapter on execution thread analysis). Problem queries that access Fat Cow tables should be re-examined by an experienced performance tuner. There may be more efficient ways of writing the original code. The proper use of expressions and operators can exploit the nuances of the optimizer and extract better performance from the system. Periodic re-examination of the code allows you to make use of knowledge and experience that you gain with your database and environment.

QUERY TACTICS AND TECHNIQUES

8

This chapter provides you with a set of query tuning techniques in a tool-kit format. You will find that a general knowledge of all of the techniques presented here will help you to write more efficient queries from the start.

Be aware that the effectiveness of some of these techniques varies based on the situation, so they work in some instances but not in others. The techniques are therefore presented with the following important recommendations:

- Know the demographic nature of your data.
- Set up a test environment that mirrors target operational environments.
- Use these techniques within your overall tuning strategies.
- Test, validate, implement and verify performance improvements.

8.1 Use >= instead of >

The expression X >= 39 goes directly to the first qualifying row, while X > 38 scans forward until 39 or greater is found. While this technique is widely known and presented in a variety of written material, our tests with System XI revealed no significant performance difference in access time on 2,000,000 rows. Note also that this tuning technique is not as effective with floating-point or character string data. However, it is still a sound coding practice and we recommend using this technique for developing portable, performance-tuned code for heterogeneous client/server systems. This practice will provide code which will run efficiently, regardless of optimizer type.

8.2 Use EXISTS and IN instead of NOT EXISTS and NOT IN

Sybase states that the use of "not" requires the Sybase Engine to scan the entire table to ensure that the value does not exist. The first instance of EXISTS will return results immediately while the use of NOT EXISTS and NOT IN would return results only after scanning the entire index or table.

When using the IN operator there are occasions where the optimizer will turn an IN into an OR clause, and this change can result in unwanted table scans.

Listings 8.1 and 8.2 show uses of NOT EXISTS and IF EXISTS.

```
use college
go
set statistics time on
Execution Time 0.
SQL Server cpu time: 0 ms.
SQL Server elapsed time: 4634026 ms.
if not exists     [Note the use of the NOT EXISTS]
(select 1 from student where last_name = "Smythe")
begin
    print "'Smythe' last name on the student table."
end
else
begin
    print "'Smythe' last name exists on the student table."
end
Parse and Compile Time 0. [see Note 1]
SQL Server cpu time: 0 ms.
```

Listing 8.1
Use of NOT EXISTS (Page 1 of 2)

```
Execution Time 0.
SQL Server cpu time: 0 ms.
SQL Server elapsed time: 3 ms. [see Note 2]
(0 rows affected)
No 'Smythe' last name on the student table.
```

Listing 8.1
Use of NOT EXISTS (Page 2 of 2)

Note 1. Normally, compile time will be reported as either a very small number or 0. However, be observant: This metric could identify whether or not you should consider using forceplan. If the compile time is a larger number, you can use forceplan to essentially "turn off" the optimizer. Compile time is then eliminated. Forceplan can sometimes shorten the optimizer's execution time. One other observation: This gives you an appreciation of how quick the Sybase optimizer is.

Note 2. Time used by NOT EXIST

```
if exists (select 1 from student where
last_name = "Smythe")  [Note the use of IF EXISTS]
begin
    goto lbl_name_exists
end
else
begin
    print "Notable."'Smythe' last name on student table."
    goto lbl_end
end
lbl_name_exists:
    print "'Smythe' last name exist on the student table."
```

Listing 8.2
Use of IF EXISTS (Page 1 of 2)

```
lbl_end:
Parse and Compile Time 0.
SQL Server cpu time: 0 ms.

Execution Time 0.
SQL Server cpu time: 0 ms. SQL Server elapsed
time: 0 ms. [0 ms with the IF EXISTS statement]
No 'Smythe' last name on the student table.

set statistics time off
Parse and Compile Time 0.
SQL Server cpu time: 0 ms.
```

Listing 8.2
Use of IF EXISTS (Page 2 of 2)

Note the execution time difference between Listing 8.1 and 8.2.

8.3 Use Parameters Vs. Local Variables in WHERE Clauses

The value of a declared variable cannot be known to the optimizer at compile time because the declared value is set in the procedure's execution. This does not apply to a parameter being passed to a stored procedure. That value is known at the start of compile time.

One way to avoid using variables is to create two procedures instead of one: The first declares the variable, and it assigns a value where there is no possible table scan cost. The second receives this value as a parameter and performs an indexed search. This technique is shown in Listing 8.3.

```
...
create procedure primary_proc
as
```

Listing 8.3
Avoiding variables by using two procedures instead of one (Page 1 of 3)

```
        declare @student numeric(10) [Notice the declared
    variable]
        select @student = student_id_nbr
          from payment
         having date_of_payment = max(date_of_payment)
        select last_name,
                first_name,
                major
          from student
         where student_id_nbr = @student
    return 0
    set showplan on [Showplan is executed for Primary_proc]
    exec primary_proc
    QUERY PLAN FOR STATEMENT 1 (at line 2).
        STEP 1
            The type of query is EXECUTE.
    QUERY PLAN FOR STATEMENT 1 (at line 6).
        STEP 1
            The type of query is SELECT.
            Evaluate Ungrouped MAXIMUM AGGREGATE.
            FROM TABLE
                payment
            Nested iteration.
            Table Scan. [Note the presence of a TABLE SCAN]
            Ascending scan.
            Positioning at start of table.
            Using I/O Size 2 Kbytes.
            With LRU Buffer Replacement Strategy.
    ...

    ----------------------------------------------------------------

    [Procedure last_student_payments is produced]
    use college
    create procedure last_student_payments
```

Listing 8.3
Avoiding variables by using two procedures instead of one (Page 2 of 3)

```
        @student numeric(10) [now student is developed as a
                              parameter. The parameter will be
                              passed to the stored procedure at ex-
                              ecution time. This allows the opti-
                              mizer to recognize the data value of
                              "student".]
    as

        select last_name,
                first_name,
                major
          from student
         where student_id_nbr = @student
    return 0

    ...

    QUERY PLAN FOR STATEMENT 2 (at line 5).
        STEP 1
            The type of query is SELECT.
            FROM TABLE
                student
            Nested iteration.
            Index: pk_student [Now we observe that the pro-
                               cedure uses an index]
            Ascending scan.
            Positioning by key.
            Keys are:
                student_id_nbr
            Using I/O Size 2 Kbytes.
            With LRU Buffer Replacement Strategy.
```

Listing 8.3
Avoiding variables by using two procedures instead of one (Page 3 of 3)

8.4 When Using Multiple Expressions, the Most Limiting Expression Should Go First

The most limiting expression should go first in an expression.   While some authorities have sighted that this is less important in the more current optimizers, and independent tests seem to indicate that this is indeed the case, we still recommend it as a good practice. Other DBMS optimizers may still be served by this rule, and use of this technique facilitates code portability in a heterogeneous client/server environment.

It should be noted that this technique assumes that all columns are indexed and the operators are the same (for example, both expressions using an = operator).

When these two conditions are not met, then the optimizer may not be able to choose the better index. For example:

```
select * from student
where last_name = "Foster" and first_name = "Daniel"
```

Since last name is generally more selective, it should go first.

8.5 Optimize ORDER BY

Make sure any ORDER BY ties specifically to a WHERE clause argument. The goal of this technique is to prevent the optimizer from executing two separate operations: the data extraction and the sort. To use this technique, create a "fake" clause. For example, in a character string use a blank string comparison:

```
Select *
from student
where last_name >= ' ' and
    date_of_birth >='1/1/60'
order by last_name
```

Notice how the ORDER BY clause ties directly to the last_name SARG. Here the selection will retrieve all rows indexed on last_name and remove all rows with birth dates in 1960 and above. This solution takes advantage of the index to "presort" the data. The alternative would cause the data extraction based on something other than the intended key followed by a sort in a separate operation.

8.6 Use Caution With the LIKE Operator

The LIKE operator is quirky. Given different situations, it is difficult to determine consistent optimization across Systems 4.9.2, System X and System XI. In Sybase version 4.9.2, the use of LIKE before a SARG always causes a scan. However, placing the SARG before the LIKE may cause use of an index instead of the scan. If the first character of the search is a "%" or "_", however, you will always get a table scan.

If you use a LIKE, then you must use Showplan to ensure it has not caused an undesirable scan.

8.7 UNION vs. OR

Use OR rather than UNION when the SARG columns are unindexed and the code references only one table. This advice is the opposite of what you would naturally assume. You cannot have indexes on every column, so when you have an access where there are no indexes the OR is preferable to a UNION.

However, with indexed columns UNION can sometimes outperform OR because the indexes may be ignored for the OR but will be used in the UNION.

In the case of OR, always use "set statistics time on" and do showplan analysis.

8.8 Avoid NOT EQUALS, !=, !>, !< and <>

Convert NOT logic into positive logic. For example, "not equals" could be converted into a matched set of > and < expressions. Don't forget that if the resulting data set size is 20% or more of the total data size, it will perform a table scan, regardless of indexes.

Conversion of NOT logic into positive logic requires knowledge of the domain. For instance "column != 100" can be converted into "column between 1 and 99 and column between 101 and 1000" if the domain of the column is 1 to 1000.

Example:

```
use college
set showplan on
select grade from grade
  where grade is not NULL  [Note the use of "is not"
                                equivalent to <>]
QUERY PLAN FOR STATEMENT 1 (at line 1).
    STEP 1
        The type of query is SELECT.
```

```
FROM TABLE
    grade
Nested iteration.
Table Scan.    [which gives you the TABLE SCAN]
Ascending scan.
```

    . . .

8.9 Convert NOT EXISTS to EXISTS

The EXISTS (or IN) clause with a subquery always performs many times faster than NOT EXISTS (or NOT IN). If you have two separate groups of code that get executed based upon a NOT EXISTS test, you can reverse them and use the EXISTS code instead. For example:

```
if not exists (subquery)
    statement 1
else
    statement 2
```

is the same as:

```
if exists (subquery)
    statement 2
else
    statement 1
```

8.10 USE NOT EQUALS When There is Not an Index

In a table where it is known that the record volume will never grow beyond several hundred records you should never use the index. Since it is going to scan regardless the use of NOT EQUALS has no ill effect.

8.11 Put the Least Restricting Expression First in OR Expressions

Putting the least restricting OR clause first is called "short circuiting." If the first clause is true, you do not need to perform the second one. Therefore, you want to put the clause which will return the most rows first because you can save processing for all of these rows.

8.12 Avoid the Danger of a Calculation in the WHERE Clause

The optimizer may not deal with calculations in an efficient way. Therefore, when possible, the best thing to do is to place calculations in the application, not as part of a query. Most DBMSs appear to perform the calculation for each row fetched: This wastes CPU time and slows performance considerably. Use the DBMS for what it is good at: fetching rows.

For example, the statement:

```
select count(*) from grade
  where grade/40*100 > 90
```

uses a table scan. In contrast, the statement:

```
select count(*) from grade
  where grade > 36
```

uses a clustered index.

8.13 Try to Use the Whole Index, or as Many Index Columns as Possible

In some cases, you may believe that the optimizer should be using an index or indexes that it has chosen not to use. In these cases, you want to force the optimizer to use the index. If you are using System XI, the easiest way to accomplish this is to use the "index" clause in the SELECT statement to force the use of the index you think will help. After making the change, use Showplan and Statistics Time to test your theory and verify that the index really makes a difference.

8.14 Always Include the Leading Portion of the Index

If the first field of an index is not specified in a WHERE clause, then the optimizer will ignore the whole index. Always include the first field of an index in the WHERE clause.

8.15 Avoid the Use of Incompatible Datatypes Between Columns

Variable length character fields (varchar) and character fields are treated by the optimizer as two separate datatypes. Also watch out for numeric (and decimal) fields that have different scale and/or precision. Some incompatible datatypes are converted by the optimizer, and most are rejected as SARGs and cause a table scan. Also watch for this with parameters passed to stored procedures.

Note that earlier releases of SQL Server had datatype incompatibilities with money and numeric values with no dollar sign indicated. This seems to be fixed in System XI.

In the following example, "125%" is a character datatype with a wild card. Tuition_amt is money. In order to use these two incompatible datatypes you must force a convert. The result is annotated below.

```
use college
set showplan on
select * from tuition
 where ltrim(convert(char, tuition_amt)) like "125%"
QUERY PLAN FOR STATEMENT 1 (at line 2).
    STEP 1
        The type of query is SELECT.
        FROM TABLE
            tuition
        Nested iteration.
        Table Scan. [Note the presence of a TABLE SCAN]
        Ascending scan.
        Positioning at start of table.
        Using I/O Size 2 Kbytes.
        With LRU Buffer Replacement Strategy.
    student_id_nbr calender_year quarter      tuition_amt
    ------------------------------------------------------------
        7407220001   1996          winter '     1,250.00
        7507220001   1994          winter       1,250.00
        7509020001   1993          autumn       1,250.00
        7509220001   1993          autumn       1,250.00
```

Listing 8.4
A table scan results from incompatible data types (Page 1 of 2)

7512180001	1994	autumn	1,250.00
7603140001	1993	autumn	1,250.00
7604010001	1993	autumn	1,250.00
7811250001	1996	winter	1,250.00
7501020001	1995	summer	1,255.00
7501020002	1995	summer	1,255.00
7501020002	1993	winter	1,256.00

(11 rows affected)

Listing 8.4
A table scan results from incompatible data types (Page 2 of 2)

Listing 8.5 shows how you could rewrite the code from Listing 8.4 in order to allow the use of money with a compatible datatype. Also note that this rethinking produced SARGs.

```
use college
set showplan on
select * from tuition
where tuition_amt >= 1250 [note the use of the >= and <=]
    and tuition_amt <= 1259
QUERY PLAN FOR STATEMENT 1 (at line 2).
    STEP 1
        The type of query is SELECT.
        FROM TABLE
            tuition
        Nested iteration.
        Using Clustered Index.    [And now the clustered
                                   index]
        Index : alt01_tuition
        Ascending scan.
        Positioning by key.
```

Listing 8.5
Modifying the where clause to avoid incompatible data comparisons (Page 1 of 2)

```
        Keys are:
             tuition_amt
        Using I/O Size 2 Kbytes.
        With LRU Buffer Replacement Strategy.
    student_id_nbr calender_year quarter       tuition_amt
    ---------------------------------------------------------
        7407220001   1996        winter        1,250.00
        7507220001   1994        winter        1,250.00
        7509020001   1993        autumn        1,250.00
        7509220001   1993        autumn        1,250.00
        7512180001   1994        autumn        1,250.00
        7603140001   1993        autumn        1,250.00
        7604010001   1993        autumn        1,250.00
        7811250001   1996        winter        1,250.00
        7501020001   1995        summer        1,255.00
        7501020002   1995        summer        1,255.00
        7501020002   1993        winter        1,256.00
    (11 rows affected)
```

Listing 8.5
Modifying the where clause to avoid incompatible data comparisons (Page 2 of 2)

8.16 Beware When Using Temp Tables

The optimizer assumes that all temporary tables have 100 rows and take up 10 pages, regardless of the actual size of the table. It uses these baseline values to determine execution plans for queries containing temp tables. These may be incorrect for your application. To circumvent this problem and let the system obtain correct statistics, create the temporary table outside the scope of the procedure that accesses it.

8.17 Avoid Datatype Inconsistencies or Modifications When Using Temporary Tables Accessed by Multiple Stored Procedures

Watch for datatype inconsistencies when referencing temporary tables that are created outside of procedures and used by multiple stored procedures (especially created by several developers). One developer can change the temp table and not notify the rest of the developers affected by the change. This problem is especially common in System 10 and above with the use of "persistent" temporary tables created by "tempdb..temptblname".

This problem can also arise when developers create persistent temporary tables to avoid asking the Data Administrator to add new tables to the regular database. Developers develop a cavalier attitude toward temporary tables; they may not realize that other developers have discovered the table and want to use it too. The original developer may feel that he can change it on a whim because it is a "temporary" table.

Clearly it is best to adopt development practices that avoid these problems.

8.18 Use "EXISTS" Instead of "COUNT(*)" When Possible

Using count(*) to do an existence check is costly. This is especially true within the body of a subquery.

When the optimizer knows that its mission is to perform an existence check, then it finds the first value and stops processing. Count(*) causes a scan of all rows.

For example, instead of this:

```
select student_name

from student

where sid < (select count(*) from department where
            blah blah...)
```

Use the following clause construct:

```
...where exists (select * from department where...)
```

Memory

One of the more obvious performance bottlenecks in database technology involves disk I/O. To combat this problem Sybase has invested heavily in time and dollars to provide System XI customers with one of the world's most sophisticated caching technologies. The use of memory caching results in faster query response time. Generally, you can cut down on I/O by storing more objects in memory.

System XI provides many new opportunities for memory customization. For example, you can assign a specific object to its own private cache, thereby relieving memory competition. In addition, you can also specify cache transfer size so that the server can retrieve more pages each time it visits the disk. In situations where data appears sequentially on a drive and you are accessing it sequentially, you can significantly lower the number of I/O requests and boost performance.

In this chapter you will learn about several techniques like these that allow you to boost system performance through the use of memory.

9.1 Total Memory Configuration Variable

As a general rule, you can boost the performance of any system by boosting the overall memory available on the server machine. You can also tune the amount of the server machine's total memory that Sybase reserves for its own use. Take as much memory as you possibly can, but do not take too much. One of two things will occur if you take too much: Either SQL Server will not start, or it will page fault. Both are undesirable.

You can calculate the amount of memory that your server requires. The server's total memory configuration variable includes the memory the server needs to run plus its overhead for internal structures. Remember that "little things" add up, and must be factored into the server memory requirements. Make sure that you include in your memory sizing requirements the number of locks, number of user connections, number of open databases, number of devices, and so on. The server's memory requirements are well documented in the user manuals for all SQL Server releases.

We recommend that you build a memory and disk map of your overall architecture. This map is important, especially in light of the new features and options which System XI provides. The map can also help you to factor in growth requirements for both memory and disk space in the future.

9.2 Data and Procedure Caches

After you have allocated as much total memory as you can, you must consider the appropriate ratio of data and procedure caches. After all the requirements of the server have been met, the rest of memory is allocated to these two primary caches. When you size the two caches, remember that they are directly proportional to one another: When you increase one, you decrease the other, and vice versa.

In a development environment, data access is not the primary concern. Instead you want to optimize the coding environment. Therefore, we recommend that you create a larger procedure cache. For production environments, you should give yourself plenty of data cache. But remember not to restrict the procedure cache's size too severely, especially if you have very large stored procedures. When you are using nested procedures, all the nested ones must fit in the cache at once.

Sybase's default is 20% procedure cache, 80% data cache. Begin with these numbers and tune up or down depending on your environment and your own volume requirements. Production environments vary greatly depending on the volume, hit rate, and size of stored procedures. You should involve your

DBA in this process and try different cache percentages looking for the best performance possible.

Sybase recommends that you estimate procedure cache size by multiplying the maximum number of concurrent users by the size of the largest stored procedure, and then adding a 25% sponge factor. To calculate stored procedure size, remember that the text of the stored procedure plus its query plan is loaded into memory. Sybase estimates that a query plan is about 25% of the size of its stored procedure's text.

To calculate the size of the largest stored procedure, use the following rule: Sybase stores the text of the stored procedure in lines of 255 characters. Eight lines can therefore fit on a page. Use the following formula provided by Sybase to figure out the size of the stored procedure's text, in number of pages:

```
select (count(*) /8) +1
    from sysprocedures
    where id=object_id("name")
```

(SQL Server Performance Tuning Guide, System XI).

9.3 Named Caches

After you have increased total memory size and allocated it properly, the most important thing you can do to optimize memory usage in System XI is to create named caches for frequently accessed objects. You can divide the data cache into several private caches. These private, or named, caches isolate an object into its own cache. This isolation reduces cache competition among objects. A table's pages will only be swapped out by other pages from the same table if the table has a private cache.

Frequently accessed lookup tables that are relatively small can use their own cache. Size the cache such that the entire table fits in memory to guarantee fast access time.

Note that you must make wise choices with regard to the objects meriting their own cache. If you allocate specific cache space to a table that does not truly need it, some other part of the system will suffer. Often the results of a poor allocation strategy will present themselves in odd places. For example, a query which looks like it should perform well will be slow. This sort of effect occurs when the important query's pages swap out too soon because there is not enough room in the cache it uses. It is therefore better to use named caches sparingly. Pick just a few tables in need of a performance boost and assign to them a named cache. Benchmark before and after the change and note any improvements or degradations.

Named caches can also help to parallelize locking on hardware with multiple CPUs. Each cache uses a spinlock to control access while writes are performed. A spinlock is so named because other processes "spin" in a tight loop while they wait for access. If you have only one cache, you have only one spinlock and contention can result in a performance degradation. Multiple caches reduce the probability of this type of contention. One CPU can access a named cache while another CPU accesses the default cache.

When creating named caches, you can pick candidate tables by concentrating on the following:

- Tables with heavy activity of all kinds, both selects and modifications
- The transaction log
- Tempdb for applications requiring numerous temporary tables, especially persistent ones
- Frequently accessed lookup tables that can remain completely in memory because they are small

9.4 I/O Size

Increasing I/O size often increases the effectiveness of a physical disk hit. When the server has to go to disk, it can read multiple contiguous disk pages almost as quickly as it can read one. Instead of having eight separate page hits, The server can access eight pages at once if the I/O size is set to eight.

Increasing I/O size only works when the server is planning to grab contiguous pages anyway. Therefore you can gain a benefit from increased I/O size in the following situations:

- Table scans
- Large range searches on a clustered index
- Covered queries, because often a large part of the leaf index page is scanned
- Select Into, because it allocates many pages at once for the new table
- Text/image columns, because they can take up multiple pages

You have to keep several things in mind if large I/O is to work effectively:

- Increase overall memory
- Change data cache/procedure cache ratio if necessary
- Create a special named cache
- Use sp_poolconfig to create an I/O pool to allow large I/O (you might want to have two pools)
- Make sure the size of the pool is evenly divisible by the type of pool it is (for example, if you are creating a 4K pool, don't specify 9K as the size of the pool)

It is best to have two I/O pools when you enable large I/O. Sometimes large I/O is inefficient: You bring pages into cache that are not needed, and they take up space that another process can use. Use two pools: one for 2K or 4K reads, and one for larger 16K reads. Too many pools adds unnecessary overhead, and there will not be enough space in any one pool for the I/O needed.

9.5 Tempdb and Memory

Tempdb is space used by the server to create temporary tables, and in most environments its use is high. You should therefore do what you can to speed tempdb access. Two approaches are possible:

- Place tempdb on a separate disk and controller to remove contention. Give it as much memory as possible.
- Put tempdb on a RAM disk.

We have found that if you put tempdb either on a RAM disk or on a solid state device (which is essentially a different way of implementing a RAM disk) you can speed up sorts and worktable creations by as much as 200%. We have witnessed actual increases of 25% in the measured total performance of client/ server systems in the field.

9.6 Controlling Aging of Objects

The SQL Server optimizer has no knowledge of what is in the cache, so it cannot know which queries requiring what data will be executed in the next 5 minutes. In some cases, however, you might have a good feel for which queries will be executed frequently. You should possess this knowledge if you are the designer/developer or DBA of the system.

Sybase has exposed several of its cache aging rules. Sybase ages things based on a "least recently used" algorithm, discarding the least recently used object when memory fills. Each procedure cache has its own "MRU/LRU chain" which strings all objects together according to their last use. Data pages will progress from the MRU to the LRU side of the chain. As they hit the LRU end of the chain they transfer to disk and release their memory. A feature called the *wash marker* near the LRU end of the chain marks those pages ready for deletion. See Figure 9.1.

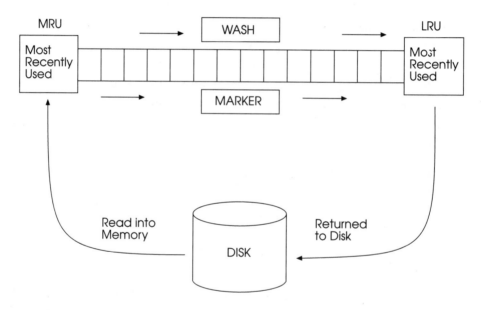

Figure 9.1

Sybase Caching Mechanisms

Data pages are not always placed at the beginning of the chain, however. If the optimizer knows that it has to read a great many pages for a query (for example, during a table scan), then it will place those pages closer to the wash marker. See Figure 9.2. These pages will therefore flush back to disk sooner than usual. This is useful because pages that are needed only once will not take up unnecessary space and cause more important, highly accessed objects to age and swap. This caching strategy is called MRU, or "fetch and discard." Show-plan will indicate whether LRU or MRU is used in any data page fetch. Fetch and discard is typically used when the optimizer is fetching many pages. Here are the typical situations where it is used:

- Range queries on a clustered index (a good place to examine for possible LRU)
- Covered queries scanning the leaf level (like !=)
- table scans (depending upon the size of the table, you might want to override this behavior, especially for lookup tables)
- Inner table joins where the table is larger than the cache
- Outer table joins where the table is larger than the cache

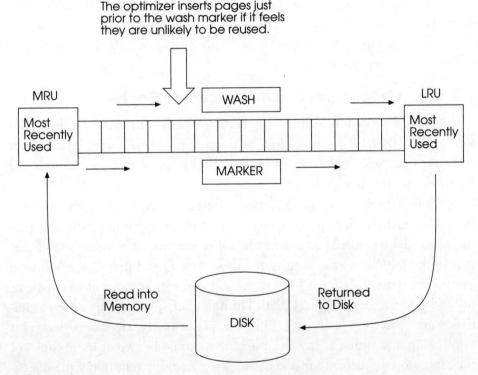

Figure 9.2
Caching Strategy for Sequentially Read Pages

The LRU strategy puts the data page at the beginning of the MRU (Most Recently Used) page chain and allows it to stay in memory until it ages properly. If a page is found in memory and read by a subsequent process, it is placed at the beginning of the MRU chain again.

Sometimes the optimizer will make the choice to use the MRU strategy, and you know that another process requires these data pages. You can force the use of LRU (or vice versa) by using the INDEX clause in the select statement. You can also force the caching strategy for write operations.

For lookup tables that you want to remain in memory as long as possible, you can use sp_cachestrategy with mru off. For instance, the department table is often used as a lookup table. Here's how to tell the optimizer NOT to use fetch and discard for the department table, with clustered index dept_index:

```
sp_cachestrategy college, department, dept_index,
    mru, "off"
```

If the table does not have a clustered index, you can specify "table only" instead of the index name:

```
sp_cachestrategy college, department, "table only",
    mru, "off"
```

9.7 Stored Procedures and the Procedure Cache

A stored procedure, when first executed, loads into cache on the MRU side of the MRU/LRU chain, along with its query plan. It ages in a manner similar to data pages in the data cache, with the exception that there is no MRU fetch and discard strategy for procedures.

Unfortunately, multiple copies of a stored procedure can exist simultaneously in cache with different query plans, and can cause unpredictable performance. Sybase stored procedures are not re-entrant. This means that if user A is in the middle of executing stored procedure Q and user B also wants to execute the same procedure Q, the server will load another copy of it into memory and generate another query plan. The new query plan will use different statistics and therefore will have different performance characteristics. This duplication means that at any given time there could be two or more copies of the same stored procedure in the cache, with very different query plans. It is not precisely known which plan the next user will get. Therefore, it is possible that the next user that executes the stored procedure will get the bad plan, and performance may suffer.

DBCC memusage will display the contents of both the procedure and data cache, and will also indicate how many copies of each stored procedure are in cache. Unfortunately, there is no way to tell what the query plans look like.

When using dbcc memusage, you must set the dbcc traceon flag first, or you will not get any output. Here's what the commands look like:

```
dbcc traceon(3604)
go
dbcc memusage
go
dbcc traceoff(3604)
go
```

9.8 Clearing Cache

There is no way that we know of to force a procedure out of memory. Procedures age in memory just like data pages that use the LRU strategy. They progress through the MRU chain until they get to the watermark and then flush.

If you have many copies of multiple stored procedures in cache, you should flush memory completely to clear out bad query plans. The only way to do this is to shut the server down and then bring it back up.

9.9 Testing and Cache Contents

Running benchmarks may superficially bias the cache in your favor, especially if you test the same query over and over. Both the procedure and the data will be in memory. Check dbcc memusage to see if the procedure is in memory. You may have to shutdown and restart the server to completely guarantee that memory is flushed so that you get accurate benchmark results.

BIBLIOGRAPHY

"Sybase Developer's Guide" by Daniel J. Worden (Sams Publishing).

"Sybase DBA Survival Guide" by Jeff Garbus, David Solomon, and Brian Tretter (Sams Publishing).

"Physical Database Design for Sybase SQL Server" by Rob Gillette, Dean Muench, and Jean Tabaka (Prentice Hall).

"Sybase and Client/Server Computing" by Alex Berson and George Anderson (McGraw Hill).

"Sybase Architecture and Administration" by John Kirkwood (Ellis Horwood).

"Optimizing SQL" by Peter Gulutzan and Trudy Pelzer (R&D Publications, Inc.).

INDEX